SUPER
CHUNKY
BOOK OF
FACT OR
FICTION

h

hinkler

Published by Hinkler Books Pty Ltd
45–55 Fairchild Street
Heatherton Victoria 3202 Australia
www.hinkler.com.au

© Hinkler Books Pty Ltd 2011, 2012

Authors: Bill Condon, Ben Ripley and Claire Saxby
Editor: Suzannah Pearce
Copyeditors: Susie Ashworth and Helena Newton
Cover and section illustrations: Rob Kiely
Cover design: Julie Thompson
Design: Ruth Comey and Diana Vlad
Illustrations: Brijbasi Art Press Ltd
Typesetting: MPS Limited
Prepress: Graphic Print Group

The publisher has made every effort to ensure that the facts and figures in this
book are correct at the time of publication. The publisher is not responsible for the
content, information, images or services that may appear in any books, journals,
newspapers, websites or links referenced.

ISBN: 978 1 7430 8714 5

Printed and bound in China

Freaky Fact or Fiction

They say that truth is stranger than fiction . . . but can you tell the difference?

This book contains over 600 strange and interesting stories about dinosaurs, the human body and inventions. Most of these are true, but some are tall tales; it will take a real expert to spot the difference.

Quiz yourself, your parents, your little sister or your best friend. You can record your answers by ticking one of the circles at the bottom of each page. Then, to check whether you were right, turn to the answers at the end of each section.

For extra fun, we've included our sources at the very end of each section. If you want to read more about dinosaurs, the human body and inventions or if you just want to double-check a fact that sounds crazy, the sources are a good place to begin your research.

You can start anywhere in the book and read the facts in any order. Whatever you do, get ready for hours of freaky fact or fiction fun!

DiNOSAURS

1 There were many different types of dinosaurs. Dinosaurs are usually classified by what they ate. Carnivores were meat-eaters; herbivores were plant-eaters; omnivores ate both meat and plants. During the time of the dinosaurs, there were also avian reptiles (those that could fly) and aquatic reptiles (those that lived in the water). The most dangerous of the dinosaurs were the carnivores. This group included the best-known dinosaur of all, the *Tyrannosaurus rex* (tie-RAN-uh-SAWR-us rex) – popularly known as the *T. rex*.

 ✓ **FACT**   **OR**   **FICTION**

2

Dinosaurs first appeared on Earth some 250 million years ago, in what is called the Triassic period. They were the kings of the beasts then, and remained so through the Jurassic and Cretaceous periods. They became extinct about 65.5 million years ago. We know so much about them today because throughout the world dinosaurs have left their mark in the shape of fossils, such as bones – lots and lots of bones – and also skin, claws and teeth. New information comes to light about them every year and for the millions who are fascinated by them, they remain the kings of the beasts.

 FACT **OR** **FICTION**

3 Scientists believe that in the time of the dinosaurs all the Earth's continents were joined in one super-continent known as Pangaea. This is a Greek word that means 'all lands'. Over millions of years, Pangaea broke apart and the various pieces 'drifted', before finally settling into the shape of the world we know today. The break-up meant that dinosaurs were transplanted to different lands. One reason why dinosaurs are found in so many weird and wonderful shapes and sizes is that they had to adapt and evolve to suit the climate and terrain of their new homes.

 ✓ FACT **OR** **FICTION**

4

In 1842, the word 'dinosaur' (Greek for 'terrible lizard') was coined by Sir Richard Owen (1804–1892), who also founded the Natural History Museum in London, England. Owen is also famous for identifying the existence of New Zealand's giant extinct bird, the moa. Owen even gave Queen Victoria's children biology lessons. However, he was a controversial figure in his day, with many claiming that while naming the superorder Dinosauria and identifying the moa, he failed to acknowledge the work of others in the field.

✓ **FACT** **OR** **FICTION**

5

Do you collect things like owls, footy cards or stamps? The Heyuan Museum in China collects dinosaur egg fossils. The count is over 10,000 and the museum is still collecting. This is the biggest collection of dinosaur egg fossils in the world. By the way, all of the eggs are much bigger than bird eggs (as you might have guessed).

 FACT   **OR**   **FICTION**

6 Dinosaur remains have been found in polar regions. In 1986, the first species of Antarctic dinosaur was found on Ross Island. It was a species of *Antarctopelta* (an-TARK-tow-PEL-ta), an ankylosaurid (an-KIE-luh-SAW-rid) dinosaur. These dinosaurs had heavy armour all over their bodies – probably to protect them. However, they didn't need a fluffy coat to keep warm. When dinosaurs were in Antarctica it wasn't covered in ice!

✓ **FACT** **OR** **FICTION**

Freaky Fact or Fiction

7

Professor Kylie Minno at England's Rocksford University has started teaching a course on assembling dinosaur bones for beginners. 'A child can bang together a heap of dinosaur bones very quickly,' she said. 'They just have to remember that the toe bone's connected to the foot bone, the foot bone's connected to the ankle bone, the ankle bone's connected to the leg bone, the leg bone's connected to the knee bone, the knee bone's connected to the – well, I won't go on – but you can see how easy it is.'

 FACT OR FICTION

8

Elliot is the nickname of Australia's largest dinosaur. Originally weighing as much as five African elephants, Elliot is about 95 million years old. His remains were found near Winton, Queensland, in 1999. Elliot is a sauropod (SAWR-uh-pod), a four-legged plant-eater with a long neck and a disproportionately small head compared to the rest of its body. His remains were found over a space the size of seven football ovals.

✓ **FACT** **OR** **FICTION**

9 Leading scientists now agree that a massive asteroid that fell to Earth 65.5 million years caused the extinction of dinosaurs. The asteroid that slammed into Mexico is said to have been one billion times more powerful than an atomic explosion. It created clouds that blotted out the sun for ten years. Scientists say that the asteroid crash resulted in 90 per cent of life on Earth being wiped out.

✓ **FACT** **OR** **FICTION**

10

Tyrannosaurus (tie-RAN-uh-SAWR-us) Sue is the world's most complete *T. rex* skeleton. It is named after Sue Hendrickson. In 1990, Ms Hendrickson discovered the 85 per cent complete, fully-grown specimen in the US state of South Dakota. It is estimated to be approximately 67 million years old. Sue is 12.8 m (42 ft) long – the length of a bus. Sue is now a permanent exhibit at the Field Museum in Chicago.

 ✓ **FACT** **OR** **FICTION**

Freaky Fact or Fiction

11 In 1906, the fossil remains of two previously unknown dinosaurs were found in a cave in India. They were about the same size as a cow. Scientific studies revealed that their heads had been covered in sores. Because of this they were given the name *Soreasaurus* (SAW-ree-a-SAWR-us). It was first believed that their sores had come about because they had poor eyesight and were constantly hitting their heads.

A more recent theory is that the sores may have been caused by prolonged kissing!

 ✓ **FACT** **OR** **FICTION**

12

The dinosaur commonly called *Brontosaurus* (BRON-toe-SAWR-us) is really an *Apatosaurus* (a-PAT-uh-SAWR-us). Othneil Charles Marsh named *Apatosaurus* in 1877. Two years later, he found a more complete skeleton, which he thought belonged to a new genus (animal or plant group). He named this *Brontosaurus*. Many years later, it was discovered that the *Brontosaurus* was really from the same genus as the *Apatosaurus*, but was a more mature specimen. Since *Apatosaurus* was the first name given, it is the correct term, although many people still refer to it as *Brontosaurus*.

✓ **FACT** **OR** **FICTION**

Freaky Fact or Fiction

13 The term 'dinosaur' stems from two Greek words: 'deinos', meaning 'terrible, or fearfully great'; and 'sauros', meaning 'lizard'. They were the dominant land animals for more than 160 million years. Although many of them were of gigantic size, some of the earliest species, such as the *Oldensaurus rex* (OLD-en-SAWR-us rex), were no bigger than a domestic dog. In 1962, fossil remains of the *Oldensaurus rex* were found in Italy. Small round stones were heaped near the remains. This has led scientists to think that the *Oldensaurus rex* may have been a primitive ancestor of the dog breed olden retriever.

 FACT **OR** **FICTION**

14

A research team at Rocksford University, headed by Dr John Smythe, has found evidence that the iceberg that collided with the Titanic in 1912 may have partly consisted of dinosaur bones. Dr Smythe said small bone samples found by divers at the wreck site are 'quite possibly' those of dinosaurs. He said that unlike other parts of the world where dinosaur skeletons would in time be buried in the ground, dinosaurs from the Antarctic lay on the ice and eventually drifted to sea as icebergs.

 ✓ **FACT** **OR** **FICTION**

15

Velociraptor (vel-os-i-RAP-tor), often just called raptor, was a turkey-sized animal commonly found in dry desert regions. Its remains were first discovered in Mongolia in 1922. It was a meat-eater and a fierce fighter. It had a long, stiffened tail with huge claws on its back feet, which it most likely used to attack or cling to its prey. *Velociraptor* had feathers and is closely related to today's modern birds.

 ✓ **FACT** **OR** **FICTION**

16

The name *Tyrannosaurus rex* (tie-RAN-uh-SAWR-us rex) means 'tyrant lizard king'. It is thought to have been able to eat up to 230 kg (500 lb) of meat in one bite. Scientists estimate it bit down on its prey with huge force. Most humans bite with a force of about 1207 kPa – kilopascals (175 psi – pound-force per square inch). However, researchers say the dinosaur probably bit with a force of up to 20,760 kPa (3011 psi).

✓ FACT OR FICTION

17

Compared to the rest of its body, *T. rex* had very short arms. They do not appear to have had any practical use, except perhaps to hold its struggling prey close to its chest during an attack. It is also possible that the arms had no use at all and, over millions of years, they would have completely disappeared. Snakes once had limbs, but gradually adapted to their present, sleeker form, which is much more suitable for their environment. This process of change over long periods of time is called evolution.

✓ **FACT** **OR** **FICTION**

18 The first recorded finding of dinosaur bones was made in 1862 by an Italian farmer, Alphonse Migarella, who made the discovery while ploughing a field near Florence. In a freak accident, the protruding hind leg of a *Stegosaurus* (STEG-uh-SAWR-us) pierced the sole of Migarella's left shoe, wounding his foot, and blood poisoning set in. Despite the best efforts of doctors, Migarella died a week later, making him the only known human victim of a *Stegosaurus*.

 FACT **OR** **FICTION**

Freaky Fact or Fiction

19 Artists work with paleontologists to try to figure out how dinosaurs really looked. In the 1800s, a British artist, Benjamin Waterhouse Hawkins, created the first life-sized sculpture of a dinosaur called *Iguanodon* (ig-WAHN-o-don). Waterhouse worked with paleontologist and zoologist Richard Owen who worked out the probable size and shape of the dinosaur, based on existing parts of its skeleton. Hawkins' dinosaurs were a major attraction at the London Crystal Palace Exhibition of 1853 to 1854. Before the *Iguanodon* model was finished, a dinner party was held inside it!

 ✓ **FACT**   **OR**   **FICTION**

20

Australia has its own lizard of Oz. Called the *Ozraptor* (oz-RAP-tor), it is Australia's oldest known dinosaur, probably living well over 100 million years ago. Some students found part of its tibia (leg bone) in the 1960s. For a long time it was thought that the bone was from an ancient turtle. It took another 30 years before anyone realised that it was a dinosaur bone. Its name means 'Australian plunderer'. It was a meat-eater that wasn't very big. It was about 3 m (9.8 ft) long and weighed approximately 45 kg (100 lb).

✓ **FACT** **OR** **FICTION**

21

One of the most amazing pterosaurs, or flying reptiles, was *Pteranodon* (TER-an-o-don). This was a huge animal with a wingspan of 7 m (23 ft). This is wider than any modern or extinct bird. Despite this, *Pteranodon* had a very light body – about 17 kg (37.5 lb). It must have been able to flap its wings and fly, as it had joints and muscles found in flying animals. It also had hollow bones filled with air.

✓ **FACT**   **OR**   **FICTION**

22

Protoceratops (pro-tow-SAIR-a-tops) had a sharp beak and a bony frill on the back of its neck. It also had thick bones on top of its nose and over its eyes. It walked on all fours and appears to have lived in large groups. In 1922, several skeletons were found in Mongolia. Skeletons of young *Protoceratops* have also been found, some still inside their eggs.

✓ **FACT** **OR** **FICTION**

23

Fossils of *T. rex* prey suggest it crushed and broke bones as it ate, and broken bones have been found in its dung. Mei Yong, a *T. rex* discovered in Mongolia, had the nearly complete skeleton of a *Triceratops* (try-SAIR-a-tops) still wedged in its mouth, leading scientists to believe it choked to death. In South America, *T. rex* skeletons have been found with large numbers of small bird fossils in their mouths. It is thought they may have choked on bird feathers.

 ✓ **FACT** **OR** **FICTION**

24

*J*obaria (jo-BAR-ee-a) was named after Jobar, a mythical creature of African legends. The herbivore's remains were found in the Sahara Desert in 1997 after being partially uncovered because of erosion. It is thought that *Jobaria* could rear up on its hind legs, like elephants do today. This dinosaur lived about 135 million years ago. From its very long neck to its equally long tail, it was around 21 to 23 m (70 to 75 ft) long and weighed about 18,200 kg (20 US t).

✓ **FACT** **OR** **FICTION**

Freaky Fact or Fiction

25

Giganotosaurus (JI-ga-NO-to-SAWR-us), which means 'giant southern lizard', was the longest meat-eating dinosaur. It was probably bigger than *Tyrannosaurus rex* (tie-RAN-uh-SAWR-us rex). It lived more than 90 million years ago and its fossils have been found in Argentina, South America. It walked on two legs and had enormous jaws with long jagged teeth. Its skull was as long as a tall adult human, at 1.8 m (6 ft), but its brain was very small.

✓ **FACT** **OR** **FICTION**

26

In 1878, 39 *Iguanodon* (ig-WAHN-o-don) skeletons were found in a Belgian coal mine. The job of sorting, preparing and describing the collection was given to Louis Dollo. It was not an easy job, as you can imagine. For the first time in Europe, Dollo was able to reconstruct some complete dinosaur skeletons in natural poses. He was also one of the first paleontologists to think about how dinosaurs lived, rather than just giving them a name.

✓ **FACT** **OR** **FICTION**

27

Brachiosaurus (BRACK-ee-uh-SAWR-us) was a huge dinosaur, growing up to 15.2 m (50 ft) tall and up to 26 m (85 ft) long. A plant-eater, it had a very long neck made of 14 separate, strong bones. If it stretched its neck up, it would be tall enough to look over a three-storey building of today. It also had very long front legs and a tiny head. A female *Brachiosaurus* usually laid its eggs in lines while walking, rather than in nests. *Brachiosaurus* lived for about 100 years. Skeletons of *Brachiosaurus* have been found in Tanzania, Africa, and in the USA.

 ✓ **FACT** **OR**   **FICTION**

28

Some experts say that pieces of rotten meat lodged in its teeth must surely have given *T. rex* a very bad case of halitosis, commonly known as bad breath. On discovery of a large number of dinosaur remains in North Africa in 1991, soil studies revealed that the plant belladonna, also known as deadly nightshade, had once grown in the area. It is suspected that dinosaurs chewed on the sweet plant to get rid of the sour taste in their mouths, causing their deaths.

✓ **FACT**　　**OR**　　**FICTION**

Freaky Fact or Fiction

29

Imagine a dinosaur that looked like a chicken! The remains of *Gigantoraptor* (ji-GAN-tow-RAP-tor), thought to have weighed 1400 kg (1.5 US t), was discovered by a Chinese professor in Mongolia, an Asian country rich with fossils. *Gigantoraptor* is the biggest bird-like dinosaur. At 5 m (16.4 ft) tall, it is about the size of *Tyrannosaurus rex* (tie-RAN-uh-SAWR-us rex). The 85-million-year-old creature is thought to have had a beak and patches of feathers. The largest known feathered animal before the Chinese discovery was Stirton's Thunderbird, which weighed 0.5 t (0.6 US t) and lived in Australia more than six million years ago.

 ✓ **FACT**   **OR**   **FICTION**

30 Like all theropods (THERE-uh-pods), *Albertosaurus* (al-BER-tuh-SAWR-us) was a fast, two-legged carnivore with short arms. It had a large head with sharp, slicing teeth and well-developed jaw muscles. It walked on its two strong legs and had bird-like, three-toed, clawed feet. *Albertosaurus* was about 9.1 m (30 ft) long, and about 3.4 m (11 ft) tall at the hips. It weighed about 2500 kg (2.8 US t) and was at one time also known as *Gorgosaurus* (GOR-go-SAWR-us). It is thought to have hunted in packs, and has been found in Asia and North America.

✓ **FACT**   **OR**   **FICTION**

Freaky Fact or Fiction

31

The *Neonasaurus* (NEE-on-a-SAWR-us) was a dinosaur that roamed the Earth some 150 million years ago. It was much smaller than its massive cousins such as *T. rex*. Because of this, it probably lived much of its life in hiding. Studies have shown that it was one of the few burrowing dinosaurs, always staying deep underground at night. If it had stayed above ground, it would have been easily seen by its enemies. The *Neonasaurus* was the only dinosaur whose skin glowed in the dark.

✓ **FACT**   **OR**   **FICTION**

32

Can you imagine a cabin built from fossilised dinosaur bones? That is what confronted paleontologist Walter Granger in 1897 in Wyoming, USA. Built by a shepherd, the small bone cabin was made from fossilised dinosaur bones of the Jurassic period. The area is now known as the Bone Cabin Quarry. It became the site of one of the most important North American finds of Jurassic dinosaur fossils. Nearby, northwest of Laramie, there is another dinosaur building. Constructed in the 1930s, the Fossil Cabin Museum contains fragments from nearly 6000 fossilised bones, some of them 150 million years old.

✓ **FACT** **OR** **FICTION**

The dinosaur *Alamosaurus* (AL-a-moh-SAWR-us) was not named after the Alamo, a famous fort in Texas, USA, as some people believe. Instead, it was named after the Ojo Alamo sandstone formation in New Mexico, USA, where *Alamosaurus* specimens were first found in 1922. Other *Alamosaurus* fossils have been discovered in Utah, Wyoming and the Big Bend region of Texas. This 21.3 m (70 ft) long reptile was the last known sauropod (SAWR-uh-pod) dinosaur, living right at the end of the age of dinosaurs. Some paleontologists think Texas may have been home to 350,000 of these herbivores.

 ✓ **FACT** **OR** **FICTION**

34

Late in 2010, scientists published amazing photos of a bird they say is the closest relative to dinosaurs ever found. And it isn't a fossil – it's a living creature! A research team exploring in the Amazon Basin discovered the bird. The size of a toucan and bright green, it has a long whip-like tail, a large crested skullcap and a small, bony horn on the tip of its nose. Scientist Thomas Bull said: 'Tests are still being done, but we are confident that this bird is the missing link. This is the big one!'

✓ **FACT**　　　　**OR**　　　　**FICTION**

Freaky Fact or Fiction

35 Ghost Ranch in New Mexico is the home of a colossal fossil bone bed. It was here in 1947 that hundreds of fossilised dinosaur skeletons were found in a jumbled grave. The fossils belonged to a dinosaur called *Coelophysis* (SEE-lo-FIE-sis). A two-legged carnivore, this creature roamed the area over 200 million years ago. It was around 3 m (9.8 ft) long and weighed about 45 kg (100 lb). And it was most likely a cannibal!

 FACT **OR** **FICTION**

36 A dinosaur called *Saichania* (sye-CHAIN-ee-uh) had its own air-conditioning system. Because it lived in a hot climate in Asia, it is thought that its nasal passages gradually adapted to allow it to moisten the air it breathed. Its name means 'beautiful one'. This refers more to the good condition of its recovered bones than its personal beauty. A herbivore, it was about 7 m (23 ft) long. Most of its body bristled with tough plates, some of them spiked. It had a bony club at the end of its tail.

 ✓ **FACT** **OR** **FICTION**

37

It is believed that all tyrannosaurs, including *T. rex*, must have been covered in feathers at some stage of their life, most probably when they first hatched out of their eggs. The largest private collection of dinosaur feathers was owned by Professor Albert Paleo, the father of paleontology, which is the study of prehistoric life. In 1840, he presented Queen Victoria with a cushion made from dinosaur feathers as a wedding gift. Today, the cushion is on display at the British Museum.

✓ **FACT** **OR** **FICTION**

38 **N**amed after the Aztec feathered-serpent god, *Quetzalcoatlus* (KWET-zal-ko-AT-lus) was a flying reptile. Bones found in the early 1970s in Texas, USA, were bigger that *Pteranodon (TER-an-o-don)* which, until then, was the largest known flying reptile. It had a wingspan of up to 15 m (49 ft) and was able to fly long distances.

It had an extremely long neck, slender jaws with no teeth and a long, bony crest on its head. Some scientists believe *Quetzacoatlus* was like a vulture and fed on the bodies of dead dinosaurs.

✓ **FACT** **OR** **FICTION**

ometimes you don't have to go out into the wilderness to find lost dinosaurs. They might be right under your nose, in a museum. This was the case when Englishman Mike Taylor visited London's Natural History Museum in 2006. A PhD student who had been studying sauropod (SAWR-uh-pod) vertebrae, he noticed a dinosaur bone that he had never seen before. Incredibly, it was later found to be a completely new species. It is called *Xenoposeidon* (ZEE-no-puh-SY-don), which means 'alien sauropod'. It had been lying unnoticed in a basement of the museum for more than 100 years.

 ✓ **FACT** **OR** **FICTION**

40

When the dinosaurs lived, there were many aquatic reptiles in the seas, such as plesiosaurs (PLEE-see-uh-sawrs), nothosaurs (NOTH-o-sawrs), mosasaurs (MO-suh-sawrs) and ichthyosaurs (IK-thee-uh-sawrs). However, these water reptiles were not dinosaurs. Another incorrect idea that people have is that hairy mammoths and sabre-toothed tigers or *Smilodon* (SMY-lo-don) lived at the same time as dinosaurs. In fact, they lived millions of years later. The mammoth became extinct 10,000 years ago and it is believed that some sabre-toothed tigers were alive just 4000 years ago!

 ✓ FACT **OR** **FICTION**

Freaky Fact or Fiction

41

It is difficult to tell if dinosaurs were smart. Usually intelligence is related to a large brain in a small body. The Cretaceous bird-like dinosaur *Troödon* (TRO-uh-don) may have been intelligent for this reason. It was a fast mover and its large eyes were equipped with stereo vision. *Troödon's* brain was relatively large and it is often listed as the smartest dinosaur. Two others that may have been a little brighter than the rest are *Deinonchysus* (dye-NON-i-kus) and *Compsognathus* (komp-sog-NAY-thus).

✓ **FACT** **OR** **FICTION**

42

Dinosaurs became extinct millions of years before the first humans lived on Earth. When Neanderthal Man did at last appear, about 120,000 years ago, dinosaur bones were scattered everywhere. Having no other materials on hand, early man sharpened these bones by rubbing them together, and then used them in the tips of arrows and spears. As well, it is believed that the first necklaces and bracelets were made from dinosaur bones.

 ✓ FACT OR FICTION

43

If you camp out in the great outdoors, you will most likely wake up to hear birds singing their morning songs. Scientists believe that dinosaurs also communicated with each other using something that might have been similar to birdsong. Many dinosaurs had complex crests that could produce low rumbles, which in some cases might have sounded like a foghorn – and we all know singers who sound like that. Another communication method might have been a mighty crack of a dinosaur tail. And finally, just as today's birds dance for their mates, it is probable that some dinosaurs danced.

 ✓ **FACT** **OR** **FICTION**

44

The arrival of *Plateosaurus* (PLAY-tee-uh-SAWR-us) marked a change in the development of dinosaurs. Before it appeared over 200 million years ago, herbivores had short necks. This made it impossible for them to reach food that was found high up in trees. Then along came long-necked *Plateosaurus*. Paleontologists believe it also had the ability to stand on its hind legs to reach trees for their food. It grew to around 9 m (29.5 ft) long and up to 4 m (13.1 ft) tall. Its name means 'flat lizard'.

✓ **FACT** **OR** **FICTION**

Freaky Fact or Fiction

In 2009, three new species of dinosaur were found in the Winton area of Queensland, Australia. The dinosaurs were given the nicknames Banjo, Matilda and Clancy. The poet Banjo Paterson is said to have written the classic Australian poem 'Waltzing Matilda' while at Winton in 1885, and he also wrote the famous poem 'Clancy of the Overflow'. Banjo is similar to *Velociraptor* (vel-os-i-RAP-tor), but is smaller. Matilda is similar to the hippopotamus of today, and Clancy is a tall animal that may have been Australia's prehistoric equivalent of the giraffe.

 ✓ FACT OR FICTION

46

In 1982, Ernst and Bobby-Sue Furphy were on a camping trip in Tupelo, Mississippi, when they accidentally made an important scientific discovery. While exploring caves in the area, they found a large mass of very old and very large bones. A research team soon identified the remains as being from a previously unknown dinosaur species. Because Tupelo is the birthplace of famous singer Elvis Presley, the Furphys named it *Presasaurus* (PRES-uh-SAWR-us).

✓ **FACT**   OR   **FICTION**

Freaky Fact or Fiction

47

ike reptiles and birds today, some dinosaurs laid hard-shelled eggs. We know this because many fossilised dinosaur eggs have been found. Some of them were in nests. The first evidence of this was in the 1920s in Mongolia when a nest of eggs laid by a *Protoceratops* (pro-tow-SAIR-a-tops) was discovered. This showed scientists that baby dinosaurs, like birds, probably stayed in their nests. Several nests have been found close together. This suggests that some dinosaurs nested in colonies. In 1869, the first fossilised dinosaur eggs were found in France. These oval-shaped eggs are as heavy as a bowling ball.

 ✓ **FACT** **OR** **FICTION**

48

Not much is known about the *Liliensternus* (LIL-ee-en-STERN-us), a dinosaur from the Late Triassic period. This is because there have been only two incomplete skeletons found. It was first found in 1934 in Germany and named after a German scientist. *Liliensternus* had a crest on its head. It was up to 5 m (16.5 ft) long, and may have weighed about 127 kg (280 lb). Scientists think it was a carnivore and might have preyed on plant-eaters.

✓ **FACT** **OR** **FICTION**

49

Imagine a terrifying monster – a 12 m (39.4 ft) long lizard – is about to eat you! If you lived in North America in the Cretaceous period, you might come face to face with the meat-eater *Acrocanthosaurus* (Ak-ro-KANTH-uh-SAWR-us). It had large spines on its backbone that it probably raised in a kind of sail. This might have been like the colourful feathers of a bird – used to warn other dinosaurs to stay away. Or it might have been used to attract a mate. *Acrocanthosaurus* fossils have been found in North America.

✓ FACT OR FICTION

50

Sometimes there is debate about whether a creature was really a dinosaur. *Dimorphodon* (dy-MORE-fo-don) is one such example. It might easily be known as 'big head', because its head was huge. It was even bigger than its body! Its neck was long and its rib cage very small. Like a kangaroo, it seems to have used its long tail to help it balance as it ran along on its two legs. This creature was actually a flying reptile, not a dinosaur as many people think. It had wings made from skin. It had two types of teeth in its jaws, which is rare for flying reptiles. Its main diet is thought to be fish.

✓ **FACT** **OR** **FICTION**

51

Dollodon (DOLL-uh-don) was a two-legged meat-eater that lived 145 million years ago. Its fossil remains were found in Transylvania, the European home of Dracula. The Transylvanians were so proud of finding the dinosaur's remains they created a toy. This toy, which was a replica of how scientists believed *Dollodon* looked, was very popular.

 ✓ FACT OR FICTION

● ●

52

There are many ways to choose a dinosaur name. Usually their names come from Latin or Greek words. Some are named after the place where they are found, such as *Argentinosaurus* (AHR-gen-TEEN-uh-SAWR-us). There are those named because of their size, such as *Megalosaurus* (MEG-uh-lo-SAWR-us) – very big – or *Bambiraptor* (BAM-bee-RAP-tor) – very small. Others are named to honour the person who discovered them, and a smaller number are named after famous people. Others still are named from what we know of their behaviour. For instance, *Velociraptor* (vel-os-i-RAP-tor) means 'speedy robber'.

✓ **FACT** **OR**   **FICTION**

53

Fossil remains of *Chirostenotes* (kie-ROSS-ten-oh-tease) have been found in Canada. This dinosaur was found in sections. First, its long, narrow hands were found in 1924. This gave it the Greek name for 'narrow hand'. Its feet were found a few years later, and its jaw was discovered a few years after that. Imagine what a job it must be for a scientist to piece all of the parts together! *Chirostenotes* had a beak, long arms with strong claws, long, thin toes and a high, rounded crest on its head – like a modern-day cassowary. Most likely it had feathers.

 FACT **OR** **FICTION**

54

Flying dinosaurs! In outer space! It sounds like a very bad Hollywood movie, but it's a fact. Dinosaurs have flown into space! The first dinosaurs in space were *Maiasaura* (may-ya-SAWR-a) and *Coelophysis* (SEE-lo-FIE-sis). In 1985, astronaut Loren Acton took a piece of *Maiasaura* bone and a piece of *Maiasaura* eggshell on an eight-day Spacelab-2 mission. In 1998, a *Coelophysis* skull was taken into space by the space shuttle *Endeavor,* which travelled to the space station *Mir.*

 ✓ **FACT**   **OR**   **FICTION**

55

Fossil remains of *Atlascopcosaurus* (AT-lus-KOP-kuh-SAWR-us) were found at Dinosaur Cove in Victoria, Australia, in the 1980s. It was a herbivore that was about 2 to 3 m (6.6 to 9.8 ft) long and was probably a fast runner. *Atlascopcosaurus* got its name from the Atlas Copco Company. This company supplied equipment for the expedition that discovered the dinosaur. Examination of a partial skeleton believed to be from an *Atlascopcosaurus* showed that in its final years the dinosaur had a severe bone infection in its tibia (shin bone), but still managed to survive for a long time while it was ill.

 ✓ FACT **OR** **FICTION**

56

An African inventor, Sh'ana Bernard, discovered fossil bones while searching for firewood in Niger in 1962. She was planning to use the bones in an invention that helped draw water from a well. However, she first showed the bones to a visiting paleontologist. Alfred Leakey identified the bones as that of a dinosaur. The new discovery was named *Afrovenator* (AF-roh-VEN-uh-tehr) in honour of Ms Bernard.

✓ **FACT** **OR** **FICTION**

Freaky Fact or Fiction

Anchiornis (AN-key-OR-nis) was a dinosaur that was only about the size of a chicken. What makes it big in the dinosaur world is the fact that it had feathers. Not only that, but scientists also now know what colour it was. While other dinosaurs had crests of bony plates and spikes, *Anchiornis* had a reddish-brown feathered crest, in a Mohawk shape. It also had a pattern of black and white stripes on its wings and feet. Its name means 'almost bird', but it is definitely a dinosaur.

✓ **FACT** OR **FICTION**

58

Clams were most likely the favourite food of *Dsungaripterus* (JUNG-gah-RIP-ter-us) from China and South America. This flying reptile had a wingspan no larger than 3 m (9.8 ft). It had an upturned upper jaw, which probably helped it snap open clams. It had no teeth at the front of its mouth, but the back contained broad, blunt teeth, which may have helped in crushing the shells. It probably also ate fish, other molluscs, crabs, insects and dead land animals. Scientists believe *Dsungaripterus* lived in colonies.

 FACT OR **FICTION**

Freaky Fact or Fiction

59

Edmontosaurus (ed-MON-tuh-SAWR-us) was a hadrosaur (HAD-ruh-SAWR), or duck-billed dinosaur. A herbivore, it weighed up to 3175 kg (3.5 US t) and was about 12.8 m (42 ft) long. Despite it size, scientists have discovered bite marks from *T. rex* on at least one *Edmontosaurus*. It was not armoured, so had little defence against bigger animals. *Edmontosaurus* had as many as 1000 teeth, but these were tiny and suited to munching vegetation, not snapping at a *T. rex*. Named for the area in Canada where it was found, *Edmontosaurus* is one of the last known dinosaurs to have lived.

 ✓ **FACT** **OR** **FICTION**

60

Chunkingasaurus (Chunk-ING-ah-SAWR-us) was so named because frozen chunks of the dinosaur were found in Antarctica. This discovery in 1932 was remarkable because all previous dinosaur remains found were fossilised bones. *Chunkingasaurus*'s meat was very well preserved. Among the remains was a stomach that contained undigested penguins, polar bears and walruses. The dinosaur body is now on display in the Natural Museum of Auckland, New Zealand.

 FACT   **OR**   **FICTION**

61

argoyleosaurus (gar-GOYL-e-oh-SAWR-us) means 'gargoyle lizard'. *Gargoyleosaurus* lived during the Late Jurassic period, about 154 to 144 million years ago, and was a herbivore. Paleontologists think that *Gargoyleosaurus* was the first true ankylosaur (an-KIE-luh-SAWR), and the smallest. These armoured dinosaurs were short and kept low to the ground. The idea of this was probably to make predators think the ankylosaur would be difficult to eat. *Gargoyleosaurus* walked on four stubby legs and was about 3 to 4 m (9.8 to 13.1 ft) long. Fossils were found in North America.

 ✓ **FACT** **OR** **FICTION**

*K*entrosaurus (KEN-truh-SAWR-us) always wore a full suit of armour. From its neck, almost to the point of its tail, it had large pointed spikes. More spikes protruded from its hips, and it had bony plates on its shoulders. No wonder its name means 'prickly lizard'. Discovered in eastern Africa, *Kentrosaurus* was less than 2 m (6.6 ft) tall and 3.5 (11.5 ft) long. A slow-moving herbivore, it was probably attacked by larger dinosaurs.

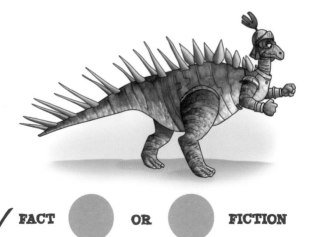

✓ **FACT**   **OR**   **FICTION**

63

Herbivorous dinosaurs are usually notable for their size. They were giants. But *Pisanosaurus* (pe-ZAHN-uh-SAWR-us) was the exception to the rule. This herbivore was only about 1 m (3.3 ft) long and 30 cm (11.8 in) tall. Not a lot is known about it because only small fragments of its remains have been found. We do know that it is one of the oldest dinosaurs, dating back to more than 200 million years ago. It was named to honour paleontologist Juan A Pisano.

✓ **FACT** **OR** **FICTION**

64

The *Telmatosaurus* (tel-MAT-oh-SAWR-us) is thought to have lived shortly before the mass extinction of the dinosaurs. One of the few dinosaurs belonging to the duck-billed dinosaur group known to have lived in Europe, its name means 'swamp lizard'. Walking on two legs, it was a plant-eater. Its height was 2 m (6.6 ft) and it was 5 m (16.4 ft) long.

✓ **FACT** **OR** **FICTION**

65

Ichthyosaurs (Ick-thee-oh-saws), meaning 'fish-lizards', were some of the largest marine animals, growing up to 10 m (about 33 ft) long. The earliest ichthyosaurs lived in the Late Triassic period, more than 200 million years ago. They were similar in appearance to the modern-day dolphin, though they were reptiles, not mammals or fish. Even though they were reptiles, ichthyosaurs gave birth to live young rather than laying eggs.

 ✓ **FACT** **OR** **FICTION**

66 Scientific studies have shown that birds are descendants of the group of dinosaurs known as theropods (THERE-uh-pods). Some of the largest dinosaurs, including *T. rex*, were theropods. However, birds came from a different, much smaller branch of the group. It is argued that since birds and dinosaurs are very distantly related, while birds still exist, dinosaurs are not really extinct. Theropods were flesh-eating dinosaurs who used their hind legs for support and movement. Their short upper limbs were probably used for grasping and tearing food. Theropod feet usually looked like those of birds.

✓ **FACT** **OR** **FICTION**

67 Have you ever wondered how dinosaur fossils are dug up? It's a job that is done very slowly and carefully. Dinosaur bones are chipped out from rock with chisels, drills and hammers. Loose rock and sand is brushed away. When the bones are ready to go to a museum, they are first sprayed with a glue to keep them strong. Then they are wrapped in bandages soaked in plaster of Paris. Or they are put into a parcel of polyurethane foam. This protects them from damage.

 ✓ FACT **OR** **FICTION**

68 The grounds of the White House in the US may hold dinosaur treasure. While patrolling the lawn area in 2010, a security guard noticed the president's dog behaving strangely. On closer inspection, he found the dog was trying to pull a bone from the ground. Tests have revealed the bone is that of a *Bambiraptor* (BAM-bee-RAP-tor). Researchers say that there may be as many as 100 dinosaurs buried near the White House. Because of this, Congress is considering whether the historic building should be demolished and rebuilt elsewhere. The President has stated that he does not wish to stand in the way of valuable research.

 FACT **OR** **FICTION**

69

*Z*uniceratops (ZOO-nee-SAIR-a-tops), the oldest horned dinosaur ever found, was discovered in New Mexico in 1996 by Christopher James Wolfe, aged eight. Christopher was with his father, a paleontologist, when he found a piece of the dinosaur's horn. The complete name of the species is *Zuniceratops christopheri* (ZOO-nee-SAIR-a-tops kris-TOFF-e-ree) – it was named in honour of its discoverer.

 ✓ **FACT**   **OR**   **FICTION**

70

A newly discovered dinosaur species – *Dracorex hogwartsia* (DRAY-koh-rex hog-WART-see-uh) – is named in honour of author JK Rowling and her Harry Potter books. The dragon-like dinosaur's name comes from the Latin word *draco* meaning 'dragon', *rex* meaning 'king', and *hogwartsia*, which stems from Rowling's fictional Hogwarts School of Witchcraft and Wizardry. Science fiction writer Arthur C Clarke has also had a dinosaur named after him, as has Michael Crichton, author of the book *Jurassic Park*.

 ✓ **FACT** **OR** **FICTION**

71

Have you ever been to a museum and seen the re-creation of a dinosaur? Museum workers wire individual fossilised dinosaur bones together and put the whole skeleton on a metal frame for display. If bones are missing, they make false bones of plaster or plastic. From marks on bones where muscles were attached, scientists can tell which bones belong where, and also how the dinosaur moved.

✓ **FACT** **OR** **FICTION**

72

$\mathbb{B}$aryonyx (bar-ee-ON-iks) looked like a large, menacing meat-eater but studies of its skull show that it was more like a fish-eating crocodile. A spinosaur (SPY-nuh-SAWR), *Baryonyx* had 30-cm-long (1-ft-long) front claws, which it may have used for catching fish, much like modern-day bears catch salmon. It was 9 m (30 ft) long and lived about 125 million years ago. Spinosaurs were a family of fish-eating dinosaurs, some of which were bigger than *T. rex*.

✓ **FACT**　　**OR**　　**FICTION**

73 efore the first dinosaurs, there were mammal-like reptiles. But when dinosaurs came, they hunted and ate the much smaller, furry animals. However, as the dinosaur population decreased, the early mammals began to multiply. When the dinosaurs disappeared, the mammals took over. Within a few million years, some of the early mammals evolved into the earliest types of horses, elephants and camels.

 ✓ FACT **OR** **FICTION**

74

After many years of research, scientists at Princedom University have concluded that dinosaurs were very itchy. It seems wherever dinosaurs lived there were always huge boulders for them to scratch themselves against. Scientists have pinpointed more than 50 of these boulders, which are still intact today. Some are more than 100 million years old. Soil samples taken from near the boulders have revealed dinosaur DNA. There are also traces of dinosaur hair and fur, as well as dandruff. The most exciting find comes from Papua New Guinea. There, scientists have discovered microscopic evidence of dinosaur fleas.

 FACT **OR** **FICTION**

75

For decades it was commonly thought that dinosaurs such as *Pentaceratops* (PEN-tah-SAIR-a-tops) and *Triceratops* (try-SAIR-a-tops) used their sharp horns and spikes to fight off predators. This may be true to some extent, but it is not their main purpose. It is now thought that the horns and spikes allowed them to recognise their own species, and to compete for mates by locking horns, much as horned animals still do today. The horns might also have been used to attract females.

✓ FACT OR FICTION

76

The fossil *Archaeopteryx* (ahr-kee-OP-ter-iks) is well known as the 'missing link' between reptiles and birds. It had feathers like a bird but its skeleton was similar to that of a small, meat-eating dinosaur. *Archaeopteryx* had feathers on its wings and tail. It could probably glide, but may not have been able to fly by flapping its wings.

✓ **FACT** **OR** **FICTION**

Freaky Fact or Fiction

77

For hundreds of years adventurers have searched for the *Doradosaurus* (dor-AH-do-SAWR-us). This name comes from the Spanish words *El Dorado*, meaning 'the golden one'. It was so named because its tail bone held heavy deposits of gold. The last major discovery of *Doradosaurus* bones was at Canada's Yukon River in 1896. A massive gold rush was triggered when news spread that the Yukon and nearby Klondike contained *Doradosaurus* graveyards. More than 100,000 people rushed there, picking the animals clean. All traces of the beast disappeared after that, but to this day scientists are still searching for the mysterious *Doradosaurus*.

✓ **FACT** **OR** **FICTION**

78 Some dinosaur bones are collected on expeditions by specialists. But amateur collectors can make great discoveries. In 1983, Bill Walker made a remarkable find – a huge curved claw. It was in a clay pit in southern England. This claw showed that it must have come from a giant carnivore that had never been found anywhere else in the world. The skull of the dinosaur was long and flat like that of a crocodile. *Baryonyx walkeri* (bar-ee-ON-iks WALL-ker-eye) was named after Mr Walker.

✓ FACT   OR   FICTION

79

Horned dinosaurs are called ceratopsian (sair-a-TOP-see-an), or horned-face dinosaurs. The biggest and most famous ceratopsian is *Triceratops* (try-SAIR-a-tops). In 2002, the remains of a dog-sized ceratopsian was discovered in China. Named *Liaoceratops* (lee-OW-SAIR-a-tops), it has two small horns, one below each eye. At 130 million years old, this creature is one of the oldest and smallest horned dinosaurs.

✓ FACT OR FICTION

80

Most of us have seen movies, such as *Jurassic Park,* in which a ferocious *T. rex* gallops alongside a fast-moving car, terrifying the passengers. Recent studies have shown that this could not have been true. *T. rex* weighed in at over 6000 kg (13,228 lb). The dinosaur would have needed most of its body weight in its legs to be able to run as fast as a car going at 72 km/h (45 mi/h). Most likely it moved slowly, so that a fast runner or a person on a bike could have escaped.

✓ **FACT** **OR** **FICTION**

81

Battles were fought over dinosaur bones. The most famous 'Bone War' took place in the United States. Two men, Edward Drinker Cope and Othniel Charles Marsh, both fossil hunters, competed against one another to find the most dinosaur bones. They fought each other and also had to fend off hostile Native Americans, who were defending their lands. This took place in the 1870s and '80s. Between them, Cope and Marsh discovered 136 new kinds of dinosaurs.

 ✓ **FACT** **OR** **FICTION**

82

A dino-snore sounds like a joke, but it really happened! Like humans, dinosaurs had soft tissue at the back of their throats. The soft tissue would silently vibrate when the dinosaurs breathed in and out. However, for some larger dinosaurs such as sauropods (SAWR-uh-pods), their giant tongues would interfere with the vibrations. When the dinosaur was sleeping, its tongue, which measured up to 1 m (3.28 ft) in length and weighed up to 150 kg (330 lb), would relax and press against the vibrating soft tissue at the back of the throat. This would cause an almighty sound . . . a dino-snore!

✓ **FACT** **OR** **FICTION**

83

Australian researchers have found evidence of what could be the world's only surfing dinosaurs. Excavations at the famed Bondi Beach in New South Wales have uncovered the fossilised remains of a new dinosaur that has been named *Dudeasaurus* (DOOD-uh-SAWR-us). This dinosaur stood on two thin legs, and had very large, flat feet – almost like miniature surfboards. *Dudeasaurus* was a strong swimmer and is thought to have 'surfed' regularly in order to catch fish. There is also a theory that the male dinosaurs may have used their surfing ability to impress female dinosaurs.

 ✓ **FACT**   **OR**   **FICTION**

84

At Danny and Dawn's Dinosaur Restaurant in Wollongong, Australia, there is a distinct dinosaur flavour. It starts with the Jurassic Parking Lot and continues with the menu. On it you will find freshly caught *T. rex* fillets, baked *Brontosaurus* (BRON-toe-SAWR-us) beans, eye of *Iguanodon* (ig-WAHN-o-don) soup and poached pterodactyl (TER-uh-DAK-til) wings. There is also a warning on the menu: Be careful! All our food has bones!

✓ **FACT**   **OR**   **FICTION**

85

ew evidence shows that Australia had its own tyrannosaur (tie-RAN-uh-SAWR), but it was a much smaller animal than its famous and ferocious relative *T. rex*. A piece of fossilised pelvic bone was actually found at Victoria's Dinosaur Cove in 1989, but was not identified as tyrannosauroid until 20 years later. Scientists say the bone once belonged to a miniature tyrannosaur with small arms and powerful jaws; it was only about 3 m (9.8 ft) long and weighed 80 kg (176 lb). This is the first evidence that the tyrannosaur family existed in Australia.

 ✓ FACT **OR** **FICTION**

86 Fossil remains have been found in India of a large snake coiled around a broken egg in a dinosaur nest. It seems the snake was about to eat a baby titanosaur (tie-TAN-uh-SAWR), when a storm or landslide hit, burying both the snake and dinosaur under a mountain of sand and mud. There they lay for 67 million years before being discovered. Other snake skeletons and dinosaur eggs were also found at the site. It is the first evidence that snakes ate dinosaurs.

✓ FACT OR FICTION

87

Scientists have now confirmed that the turkey-sized *Sinosauropteryx* (sye-nuh-SAWR-OP-ter-iks), which roamed the land of modern-day China about 125 million years ago, was covered in orange and white feathers, and had white stripes on its tail. Rather than using them for flying, camouflage or warmth, the feathers were most probably for display purposes. Professor Michael Benton from the University of Bristol said that feathered dinosaurs might have come in many colours.

 ✓ **FACT** **OR** **FICTION**

88

cientists have found that dinosaurs were the big winners when volcanic eruptions shook the world 200 million years ago. Paleontologists say the eruptions killed off the dinosaur's main rivals, the crurotarsans (crew-ro-TAR-sans). These creatures were closely related to modern-day crocodiles. Scientists still don't know why the dinosaurs survived the eruptions while the crurotarsans were destroyed.

✓ **FACT** **OR** **FICTION**

Freaky Fact or Fiction

The Chambridge Dictionary has recently added several new words to its list, and they all relate to dinosaurs. A baby dinosaur, whether male or female, is now known as a cubasaur (CUB-uh-SAWR). A mature male dinosaur is a roarasaur (RAW-uh-SAWR), while a mature female is a msasaur (MIZZ-uh-SAWR). A vicious dinosaur is a snapasaur (SNAP-uh-SAWR). And a timid dinosaur is a wussasaur (WOOSS-uh-SAWR). Finally, the collective name for a herd of dinosaurs is a thump.

 FACT **OR** **FICTION**

90 The fastest dinosaur was probably *Struthiomimus* (strooth-ee-uh-MY-mus). This animal was shaped like an ostrich, but had a long tail. Its name actually means 'ostrich mimic'. It is estimated that *Struthiomimus* could have run as fast as an ostrich or a horse. It needed to be fast because bigger dinosaurs liked to eat it. It had no teeth, just a horny beak, and some scientists think it was mainly a herbivore.

✓ **FACT**   **OR**   **FICTION**

91

Iguanodon (ig-WAHN-o-don) was a herbivorous dinosaur that lived in Europe, North America, North Africa, Australia and Asia, mostly during the Late Jurassic and Early Cretaceous periods between about 161 million and 100 million years ago. *Iguanodon* weighed as much as 4.5 t (nearly 5 US t), were about 9 m (30 ft) long, and stood up to 9 m (30 ft) tall on their hind legs. *Iguanodon*'s long, flat head ended in a horny beak, and its jaws contained teeth that looked like those of the modern-day iguana lizard. Its name means 'iguana tooth'.

 FACT   **OR**   **FICTION**

92

British fossil hunter and clergyman William Buckland (1784–1856) was the first person to scientifically describe and name a dinosaur. In 1824, he gave the name *Megalosaurus* (MEG-uh-lo-SAWR-us) to a dinosaur whose fossil remains had been found nearly 200 years before. Buckland always collected his fossils in a large blue bag, which he nearly always carried with him. At the time he named *Megalosaurus*, the word dinosaur hadn't even been invented yet.

 FACT **OR** **FICTION**

93

Megalosaurus (MEG-uh-lo-SAWR-us), which means 'great lizard', walked on two strong legs and had a massive tail. It had short arms and three-fingered hands with sharp claws. It was up to 9 m (29.5 ft) long, 3 m (9.8 feet) tall and weighed about 1 t (1.1 US t). Like *T. rex* and other large dinosaurs, it may have been a scavenger as well as a hunter. When some of its large bones were first discovered, it was thought they belonged to a giant man.

 ✓ FACT **OR** **FICTION**

Dinosaurs

94

Field tests at Hollywood University have shown that North American dinosaurs were migratory animals. It seems dinosaurs usually coped fairly well with the chilly temperatures of places such as present-day New York or Boston. However, the winter cold was too much for them. When the snows came many thousands of them would make their way to Miami and Florida, where it was much warmer. Las Vegas was also a popular destination. Scientists are almost certain this great migration began on the same day every year. This caused the world's first traffic jam.

 ✓ FACT OR FICTION

Freaky Fact or Fiction

95 Boston Professor Horace Rubble hotly disputes the theory that dinosaurs became extinct after a huge asteroid crashed into Earth. 'The real reason is that dinosaurs died off because they were bored,' Professor Rubble said. 'It is so obvious. They lived in a world where there was nothing to do but eat – and what boring foods they had! Believe me, if an asteroid had crashed into Earth the dinosaurs would have been happy. It would have given them some entertainment!'

 ✓ FACT OR FICTION

96

When dinosaur bones were first found, they were thought to be the bones of giants. The first remains that were recognised as those of huge reptiles were supposedly found by Mary Mantell in 1822. Mary apparently found fossilised teeth in Sussex, England. Her husband, Dr Gideon Mantell, studied the fossilised teeth and some bones, and decided they were like those of the iguana lizard, but much bigger. He later named the big reptile *Iguanodon* (ig-WAHN-o-don).

✓ **FACT**   **OR**   **FICTION**

Freaky Fact or Fiction

97

A 150-million-year-old landing strip for pterosaurs (TER-uh-SAWRS) was found in France in 2009. The 'runway' shows that the reptiles landed feet first, then staggered before walking on all fours. However, scientists still do not know how the pterosaurs took off. The tracks were made by small pterosaurs, which had a wingspan of 1 m (3.3 ft) and feet that were only 5 cm (2 in) long.

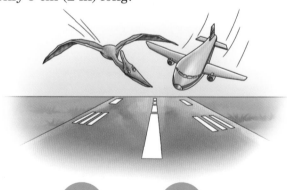

 FACT   **OR**   **FICTION**

98

Allosaurus (AL-uh-SAWR-us) was a large, carnivorous dinosaur that lived around 150 million years ago, during the Late Jurassic period. These dinosaurs reached 12 m (39.4 ft) long, stood more than 4.5 m (14.8 ft) tall and weighed up to 3.6 t (nearly 4 US t). *Allosaurus* was a biped; it walked on two stout hind limbs and had large bird-like feet, using its heavy tail for balance. It had sharp, grasping claws on its toes and on the hands of its short forelimbs. *Allosaurus* was probably a scavenger as well as a hunter, and may have hunted in groups.

✓ **FACT** **OR** **FICTION**

99

Titanosaur (tie-TAN-uh-SAWR) bones have been found on every continent in the world. Scientists have worked out that titanosaurs were giant herbivores that walked on all fours and weighed up to 100 t (110 US t). Most titanosaurs were walking fortresses. Their armour consisted of solid bony plates that covered their bodies and protected them. It is thought that titanosaurs were herd animals, often travelling in large packs. The reason why animals herd is because it offers them some protection against predators. You may have heard of the saying: 'There's safety in numbers'.

 FACT **OR** **FICTION**

100

A research team led by Professor Ian 'Edgy' Border of Camberbridge has found that dinosaur bones may prove valuable to gardeners. Microscopic analysis of *Triceratops* (try-SAIR-a-tops) bones has detected huge deposits of odium, an extremely rare fertiliser. It is estimated that the crushed bones of just one large dinosaur would provide enough odium for every garden in England. Professor Border has called for more tests to be done before using dinosaur odium as a fertiliser. 'We know it would give us giant vegetables,' he said. 'But we need to make sure it doesn't give us giant people, too.'

✓ **FACT** **OR** **FICTION**

Freaky Fact or Fiction

101 There were flying reptiles during the dinosaur era, but did birds evolve from dinosaurs? Some people believe that birds evolved from a group of reptiles called thecodonts (THEE-cuh-donts) during the Triassic period (248 to 208 million years ago.) The problem is that no good fossils of birds have been found dating back beyond about 160 million years ago, let alone to Triassic times.

✓ FACT OR FICTION

102

Coelurus (see-LOOR-us) had hollow bones and its name means 'hollow tail'. Its skull would have fit into a human hand and it was as tall as a man. It was lightly built for speed and action, and walked on its two back legs. *Coelurus* ate small vertebrate animals, such as lizards and early mammals. It lived in the forests and swamps of the Late Jurassic period.

✓ **FACT**　　**OR**　　**FICTION**

103 An almost complete skeleton of *Compsognathus* (komp-sog-NAY-thus) was found in 1972 in France. At first it was thought to have had flippers on its front feet – to help it swim. This was an amazing 'discovery'. However, further studies proved this was not so. There have only been two *Compsognathus* skeletons found. The other was in Germany, in the 1850s. Both were the size of chickens. Its name means 'pretty jaw'.

✓ **FACT**   **OR**   **FICTION**

104

Texas millionaire Bubba 'T-Bones' Jones has been sentenced to ten years jail for 'dinosaur stealing'. One day in 1990, the unemployed Jones was walking through a field when he noticed a large bone jutting up from the ground. It was a dinosaur bone! Jones quickly discovered that the whole field was littered with ancient bones. For the next 18 years, he charged people US$1000 (A$1180 or £690) a day to dig in the field. He was arrested in 2009 when it was found that he did not own the land. By that time his fortune had grown to US$13 million (A$15.3 million or £9 million)!

✓ **FACT** **OR** **FICTION**

105

People have sometimes made the wrong assumption that people and dinosaurs lived at the same time. This could be because of some films that showed this happening. One such film was *One Million Years BC* (1966). Another was *The Lost World* (1960), which sent explorers to a weird place in the South American Amazon rainforest where dinosaurs had survived. In *The Last Dinosaur*, made in 1977, some oil prospectors in Antarctica defrost a *Tyrannosaurus rex* (tie-RAN-uh-SAWR-us rex). Mention must be made, too, of *The Flintstones*, a movie and television show in which a prehistoric family had a pet dinosaur named Dino.

✓ FACT OR FICTION

106

Insects called dung beetles help droppings from large animals, such as elephants or horses, break down into soil. It is likely that dung beetles were around during the dinosaur years. They had a lot of hard work to do since one dropping from a dinosaur such as a *Stegosaurus* (STEG-uh-SAWR-us) would fill a large household garbage bin!

 FACT **OR** **FICTION**

Freaky Fact or Fiction

107

Until recently, scientists believed grass evolved after the dinosaurs. But there is now proof that some dinosaurs did eat grass, because grass remains have been found in their stomachs, and fossilised dung. However, the grass may have been really tall – perhaps as tall as a man!

 ✓ FACT   **OR**   **FICTION**

108 The *Blottosaurus* (BLOT-uh-SAWR-us) was unique to a small section of the Gobi Desert. Similar in height and shape to the giraffe, this long-necked dinosaur lived entirely on jungle juice berries found high up in sauropod (SAWR-uh-pod) trees. The berries contained a small amount of alcohol. Since the *Blottosaurus* ate them day and night, scientists believe they may have often been intoxicated. It is suspected that the sauropod trees could have been destroyed by the *Blottosaurus* during a drunken rampage, leaving them nothing to eat. If so, this means the *Blottosaurus* is the only dinosaur that wiped itself out.

✓ **FACT** **OR** **FICTION**

Freaky Fact or Fiction

109

The first dinosaurs lived in a very different environment to the modern world. At the time of the first dinosaurs there were no flowering plants. There were giant forests with trees such as cycads, conifers, ferns and gingkoes. The first flowering plants, such as passion flowers and magnolias, appeared in the Cretaceous period. Other flowers such as buttercups came later. In 1989, one of the oldest known flowers was discovered in 115- to 118-million-year-old rocks at Koonwarra in South Gippsland, Australia.

 ✓ **FACT** **OR** **FICTION**

110

Most people know that flamingos get their pink-coloured feathers from eating crustaceans (such as prawns or shrimp). Millions of years before flamingos existed, *Pterodaustro* (ter-o-DAWS-tro) had very bristly teeth in its bottom jaw. It may have used these like a sieve, to filter out small animals such as crustaceans from mouthfuls of water. Perhaps this flying reptile was pink like a flamingo!

 FACT **OR** **FICTION**

Freaky Fact or Fiction ● ● ● ● ● ● ● ● ● ● ● ●

111

In 2006, American paleontologist Anthony Martin found the first evidence that dinosaurs burrowed in the earth. While working in Montana, USA, Martin discovered three small dinosaurs in an ancient fossilised burrow. A year later he was in Australia. He had gone to an isolated area called Knowledge Creek, in Victoria, to search for dinosaur tracks. Yes, he did find dinosaur tracks that day. Incredibly, he also found three more dinosaur burrows. The Australian find is said to be about 106 million years old, making it 11 million years older than the US discovery.

 FACT   **OR**   **FICTION**

112 It had long been thought that the first feathered dinosaurs lived some 150 million years ago. This changed in 2009 when the discovery of *Tianyulong confuciusi* (tee-AN-yu-long con-FUCE-us-ee) was announced. A small herbivore about the size of a cat, this feathered dinosaur lived about 198 million years ago. This means that it, and perhaps other feathered dinosaurs, might have lived when dinosaurs first appeared on Earth. The fossil remains of *Tianyulong confuciusi* were discovered by a team of Chinese scientists. Now scientists are excited about the possibility of finding other 'feathered friends'.

✓ **FACT** **OR** **FICTION**

Freaky Fact or Fiction

113

In May 2010, a team of American paleontologists announced the discovery in Mexico of a new dinosaur species: *Coahuilaceratops magnacuerna* (kow-WHE-lah-SERA-tops mag-NA-KWER-na). This beast was a giant herbivore that lived 72 million years ago. Its most notable features are two massive horns above its eyes. At 1.2 m (4 ft) long, they are the longest horns of any known dinosaur. Scientists say little is known about the dinosaurs of Mexico, so this find is both exciting and important. What is just as exciting is that more dinosaur fossils are expected to be found in Mexico in the future.

 ✓ **FACT** **OR** **FICTION**

114

For 200 years, a box of ancient bones was stored in a forgotten cabinet at the Rome Dinosaur Centre. Until 2007, no-one even realised the bones were there. When they were finally rediscovered, the centre's leading scientist, Professor Mort Adello, knew it was an exciting find. DNA tests showed that this dinosaur was highly intelligent. The female of the species even allowed her young to shelter under her during storms. Professor Adello had no trouble thinking up a name for the new species. He called it *Umbrellosaurus aperiri* (um-BRELL-uh-SAWR-us AP-er-IR-ee).

✓ **FACT** **OR** **FICTION**

Freaky Fact or Fiction

115

Most teens eat a lot. They also have growth spurts when they get taller and put on weight. But there has never been a teen who could match the eating habits or the growth spurts of *Tyrannosaurus rex* (tie-RAN-uh-SAWR-us rex). Studies show that between the ages of about 14 and 18, *T. rex* gained around 2.07 kg (4.6 lb) every day! Because of its monster appetite it reached a weight of about 5 t (5.5 US t) by the time it was 20. By then its eating had slowed. It is thought to have lived to its late 20s.

 ✓ **FACT**   **OR**   **FICTION**

116

Imagine walking in an area so thick with dinosaur eggshells that you can't avoid stepping on one and shattering it. That's what scientists faced when they made one of paleontology's most amazing discoveries in 1998. In a desert in Argentina was a vast dinosaur nesting ground. It covered 2.6 km² (1 mi²) and on it were scattered thousands of dinosaur eggs. It is thought the dinosaurs were titanosaurs that lived 70 to 90 million years ago. Fossilised skin found inside the eggs is scaly and similar to that of modern-day lizards.

✓ **FACT** **OR** **FICTION**

Freaky Fact or Fiction

117

For decades *Velociraptor* (vel-os-i-RAP-tor) has had a reputation as a particularly cruel dinosaur. It had a knife-like claw on its second toe, which many thought was used as a vicious weapon. New research shows that this claw was probably used to hold the prey rather than to kill it. An English scientist even built a mechanical copy of the claw to test how lethal it would have been. He found it could pierce skin, but would have been too blunt to tear open, or disembowel, a victim. Further studies show that the claw might have been used to help *Velociraptor* climb trees.

✓ **FACT** **OR** **FICTION**

Dinosaurs

118

Believe it or not, the mighty dinosaur was once attacked by animals about the size of squirrels. No, they weren't really brave squirrels – the dinosaurs were already dead! In 2010, American paleontologists, Nicholas Longrich and Michael J. Ryan were studying museum specimens when they found tooth marks in some dinosaur bones. They were able to tell from the teeth mark patterns that they were made by extinct squirrel-like mammals. Longrich and Ryan said it is likely the animals chewed on the bones much the same way people eat corn on the cob. The bones were more than 70 million years old – your corn cob probably won't last that long!

✓ **FACT** **OR** **FICTION**

Freaky Fact or Fiction

119

A recent discovery has allowed scientists to look inside a dinosaur's brain for the first time. In 2008, a polar research team found a *Brachiosaurus* (BRACK-ee-uh-SAWR-us) buried under a mountain of ice at the South Pole. The bones of the 24-m-long (79-ft-long) beast were scattered in thousands of pieces. Its bodily organs had been eaten by polar bears. However, its head lay under a boulder so that bears could not reach it. The extreme cold protected the brain from decay. Tests are still in progress at the Albert Einstein Dinosaur Academy in Paris.

✓ **FACT** **OR** **FICTION**

● ●

120

Maiasaura (may-ya-SAWR-a) means 'good mother lizard'. These dinosaurs made their nests together and lived in very large herds. They dug man-sized holes into the ground to make the nests which they then filled with about 25 eggs. The *Maiasauras* grew to just over 9 m (30 ft) in length. They must have been good planners, because their nests were about this distance apart. Evidence suggests that they cared for their young, which is how they got their name.

 ✓ **FACT** **OR** **FICTION**

121

Dinosaur eggs came in all sorts of sizes and shapes. The egg of a *Velociraptor* (vel-os-i-RAP-tor) was long and thin. It had a pointed end, with lots of short ridges on the shell. It was about twice the size of a chicken egg. A *Hypselosaurus* (HIP-sih-luh-SAWR-us) egg was as big as a football and oval-shaped. The horned plant-eater, *Protoceratops* (pro-tow-SAIR-a-tops), laid a long, thin egg with bumps on it. Much larger was a sauropod (SAWR-uh-pod) egg. It was oval-shaped and the shell was covered in small bumps and short ridges.

 ✓ **FACT**   **OR**   **FICTION**

122

Tails were very important for dinosaurs. Sauropod (SAWR-uh-pod) dinosaurs, like *Diplodocus* (di-PLOD-uh-kus), often used their tails for balancing. By rearing up and leaning on their hind legs and tails, they could reach into the treetops for their food. Fast moving, two-legged dinosaurs used their tails for balance when they ran. Others used their tails for self-defence when they were under attack.

✓ **FACT** **OR** **FICTION**

Freaky Fact or Fiction

123 All the dinosaurs that used their tails to protect themselves had four feet and ate plants. Some scientists think some dinosaurs used their tails as a kind of whip, which may have caused a stinging pain to large meat-eaters. Anklyosaurs (an-KIE-luh-SAWRS) and stegosaurs (STEG-uh-SAWRS) had clubs and spikes on their tails, which they probably used to hit their enemies and cause terrible wounds.

✓ FACT OR FICTION

124

A 'dinosaur dance floor' – that's what scientists are calling an oasis on the border of Arizona and Utah in the USA. This is where they found more than 1000 dinosaur footprints in 2008. They say the area was most likely a watering hole amid desert sand dunes during the Jurassic period, 190 million years ago. The tracks once were thought to be potholes formed by erosion. They are near a popular wind-sculpted sandstone formation known as The Wave.

 ✓ **FACT** **OR** **FICTION**

Freaky Fact or Fiction

125

Scientists from the Albert Einstein Dinosaur Academy have released a report on their study of 'Bobo', a *Brachiosaurus* (BRACK-ee-uh-SAWR-us) found with its brain intact. A team of 50 worked on the study, and the two-year project cost US$1.9 million (A$2.2 million or £1.3 million). Using Electrical Impulse Analysis, they learnt that from 7 am to 7 pm, Bobo thought of food. The dinosaur slept for at least 12 hours, but even then his mind was active. All night long, he thought of food.

 FACT **OR** **FICTION**

126

Dinosaurs had all kinds of teeth. Some teeth were smaller, but much sharper, than human teeth. Some teeth were used to hook into the dinosaur's victims. Many teeth were huge, especially those of meat-eaters. These dinosaurs' teeth kept growing and were constantly replaced during their lives. Some of the large teeth had jagged edges, like the serrated edge of a steak knife. A large number of plant-eaters swallowed rocks, known as gizzard stones, to help them grind up plant fibres.

✓ **FACT**   **OR**   **FICTION**

127

Fossil hunters in Brazil have discovered what could be the first complete family of dinosaurs. The bones of nine dinosaurs were found huddled together in 2009. This suggested that they may have been related. Now, through laser dating, a definite pattern has emerged. There are five young dinosaurs. These are believed to be the family's 'children'. Then there is a mature male and a mature female. These could be the parents. Finally, there is a much older male and a much older female. They are most likely the grandparents. Only one dinosaur has been named as yet. The oldest female is *Grannysaurus* (GRAN-nee-SAWR-us).

 ✓ **FACT** **OR** **FICTION**

128

Have you ever wondered just how many dinosaurs there were? So far scientists have found over 300 genera (general groupings). Within each genus there can be many different species. Most of them ate plants, and about 100 kinds ate meat. The biggest dinosaurs were plant-eaters, weighing about 90.7 t (100 US t) and measuring 33.5 m (110 ft) long. The biggest carnivores were 8 t (8.8 US t) and 13.7 m (45 ft) long.

✓ **FACT** **OR** **FICTION**

Freaky Fact or Fiction

129

Triceratops (try-SAIR-a-tops), which means 'three-horned face', belonged to a group of dinosaurs known as ceratopsians (sair-a-TOP-see-ans), or horned dinosaurs. When *Triceratops* was first found in North America, it was wrongly described as a bison! *Triceratops* had three horns: one on its nose and two long ones above its eyes. It had a short neck frill and was heavily built, with strong legs. It was large and about 9 m (29.5 ft) long.

 ✓ **FACT** **OR** **FICTION**

130

Some fossils are worth a lot of money, not just because they are from the time of the dinosaurs, but because they are partly made out of precious stones called opals. An opalised jawbone with teeth from *Steropodon galmani* (stair-OP-uh-don gal-MAHN-ee) was found at Lightning Ridge in New South Wales, Australia. It was one of the earliest monotreme (egg-laying mammal) fossils found in Australia. The opalised skeleton of a marine reptile, known as the 'Addyman plesiosaur' (PLEE-see-uh-SAWR), was found in 1968 by opal miners in Andamooka, South Australia.

 ✓ **FACT** **OR** **FICTION**

131

Some dinosaurs got diseases that people get today. It seems amazing, but it's true. Fossilised dinosaur bones have shown swollen areas of tumour growth. This is a sure sign that the animal suffered from cancer. In North America, a scientific team used an X-ray machine to scan 10,000 dinosaur bones. They found tumours in the bones of hadrosaurs (HAD-ruh-SAWRS). Hadrosaurs, or duck-billed dinosaurs, were plant-eaters from the Cretaceous period, about 70 million years ago.

 ✓ FACT OR FICTION

132

In South America today there lives a hoatzin (waht-SEEN) bird, which has claws on its wings. Baby hoatzins use their claws to climb tree branches. The prehistoric flying creature, which also had claws, was *Archaeopteryx* (ahr-kee-OP-ter-iks). *Archaeopteryx* was the earliest known bird. It appeared in the Jurassic period. It had a tooth-filled head and a long, bony tail like a dinosaur.

✓ **FACT**   **OR**   **FICTION**

Freaky Fact or Fiction

133

Studies of a cave deep in Egypt's Sahara Desert have shocked the scientific world. Using the latest super-density acoustic equipment – an acousticator – scientists have heard the faint but distinctive roars of a dinosaur! It is believed the beast was roaring at the very moment a tremendous sandstorm buried the cave's entrance. The dinosaur and its roar remained trapped for 150 million years. A digital music download of the roar is expected to go on sale by Christmas 2011. All proceeds will go to the Society for the Advancement of Dinosaurs.

 FACT **OR** **FICTION**

134

hen scientists find fossils of dinosaur bones, they need to free the bones from the rock they are in. If they chipped them away, they might damage the bones and it would take a very long time. So the fossilised bones go to a laboratory still inside the rock. There they dip the fossil into a vat of acid. This frees the fossil from the rock without damaging it. The chemicals used are very dangerous so workers need to use protective clothing.

 ✓ **FACT** **OR** **FICTION**

Freaky Fact or Fiction

135

Hypsilophodon (hip-sih-LUH-foh-don) remains were first found in England in 1849. Its name means 'high crested tooth'. *Hypsilophodon* had about 30 ridged or uneven teeth which probably ground against each other, which meant they were self-sharpening. Initially some scientists thought that because of its size this plant-eating dinosaur lived in trees to protect it from bigger predators. However, it was very much a ground-dweller. At 2 m (6.5 ft) in length but only waist-height on a modern man, it was small for a dinosaur, but very quick on its feet. Because many fossils of *Hypsilophodon* have been found in one place, it is suspected that it travelled in herds.

✓ **FACT** **OR** **FICTION**

Dinosaurs

136 The Chinese have been collecting dinosaur fossils for over 2000 years. They used to refer to them as 'dragon's teeth', because it was mostly dinosaur teeth that they found. Thought to have healing powers, the bones were ground into powder. It seems likely that the mythical Chinese dragon, an important symbol in Chinese culture, might have originated from the discovery of dinosaur remains.

✓ **FACT** **OR** **FICTION**

Freaky Fact or Fiction

137

Dinosaurs can be split into two groups according to their hipbones. They are the saurischians (sawr-RISS-kee-ans), or lizard-hipped dinosaurs, and the ornithischians (or-ni-THISS-kee-ans), or bird-hipped dinosaurs. All meat-eating dinosaurs were lizard-hipped, but some plant-eaters were also lizard-hipped. Ornithischians were all plant-eaters. Scientists believe that birds have evolved from lizard-hipped dinosaurs, not bird-hipped dinosaurs. Isn't that strange?

✓ **FACT** **OR** **FICTION**

138

Living in the area of the Gobi Desert in Mongolia about 80 million years ago was the *Oviraptor* (oh-vee-RAP-tor). The first skeleton of this dinosaur was found in 1923, supposedly near a nest of *Protoceratops* (pro-tow-SAIR-a-tops) eggs. So it was thought that *Oviraptor* was an egg-eater. It had an oddly shaped toothless beak and stood about 2 m (6.6 ft) tall. Its name is Greek for 'egg thief' because it was first thought that it had stolen the *Protoceratops* eggs. It is now thought the eggs probably belonged to *Oviraptor*.

 FACT OR **FICTION**

Freaky Fact or Fiction

139

While helping to build a school vegetable garden in Queensland, Australia, a boy found remnants of a prehistoric creature. In 2010, the Year 8 boy struck what he thought was a rock, when planting vegetables. An alert teacher took a closer look and realised the rock was actually a fossilised bone from an ichthyosaur (IK-thee-uh-sawr). It was about 100 million years old. But there was still one more ancient treasure in the vegie patch. Under the bone was a book that had been borrowed from Brisbane Library in 1904!

 ✓ **FACT** **OR** **FICTION**

140

Englishman Samuel Johnson wrote one of the first dictionaries. Words were Johnson's hobby, but he had another one as well. When he wasn't searching for new words, Johnson loved searching for dinosaur fossils. Every weekend for many years, he set off for the country with little more than a map, some food and a shovel. He nearly always came back empty-handed. But then, in 1723, he discovered a dinosaur that no-one had ever seen before. Johnson's son Theo was always called 'The', so he named the new dinosaur in his honour. You may have heard of a *Thesaurus* (thuh-SAWR-us).

✓ FACT OR FICTION

Freaky Fact or Fiction

141

Some people believe a dinosaur called Loch Ness lives today in a lake in Scotland. They have described the Loch Ness Monster as looking like a plesiosaur (PLEE-see-uh-sawr). This would make 'Nessy' a very old monster because plesiosaurs have been extinct for 65 million years. As well, even though plesiosaurs were water dwellers, they were air-breathing reptiles. This means that 'Nessy' would be regularly coming up for air and, no doubt, having her photo taken.

 ✓ FACT OR FICTION

142

Which were the fastest dinosaurs? Fossil footprints give the best information about how fast a dinosaur could move. Small dinosaurs were best suited to bursts of speeds over long distances. They usually had light skeletons and long limbs, feet, toes and claws. The small to medium coelurosaurs (SEE-loor-uh-sawrs), such as ornithomimosaurs (or-nith-uh-MIME-uh-sawrs) and dromaeosaurs (DROME-ee-uh-sawrs), were probably the fastest of all dinosaurs. Scientists have worked out that some species could run faster than 64 km/h (40 mi/h).

 ✓ **FACT** **OR** **FICTION**

143 Dinosaurs ruled the Earth for over 150 million years. This makes them the most successful group of backboned animals to have ever lived on land. Compare this with the human race – somewhere between four million and six million years! An insect that has outlived dinosaurs – and will probably outlive humans – is the cockroach. In fact, the fossil of a giant prehistoric cockroach has been found in North America. This cockroach was scuttling around on Earth 55 million years before the dinosaurs arrived.

✓ **FACT** **OR** **FICTION**

144

Early explorers may have been the only humans to actually see living dinosaurs. In 2010, marine archeologists in Greenland found the log of an ancient Viking ship. Drawings in the log showed creatures that are almost identical to *Hadrosaurus* (HAD-ruh-SAWR-us). Professor Vivian Moss of Ivy University said this finding has excited scientists. 'This could prove that some dinosaurs survived extinction by taking to the water,' she said. 'Certainly they eventually became extinct, but they may have lived much longer than we currently think.'

✓ **FACT**   **OR**   **FICTION**

Freaky Fact or Fiction

145

There are different kinds of fossils. Some can be animals or plants preserved in plant sap or resin (amber). Or they can be preserved in peat bogs and tar pits when they have turned into 'mummies' or have been frozen. Another type of fossil is where the living tissue has been petrified, or turned into stone. Finally, a fossil can be created when the original remains have dissolved and left a mould. This is filled with minerals such as quartz.

✓ **FACT**   **OR**   **FICTION**

146

The central region of South Africa is where many prehistoric fossils have been found. The most common plant-eaters from this area were the dicynodont (die-SIGH-no-dont). These pig-shaped mammal-like reptiles had just two canine teeth in their upper jaw. Their name means 'two dog toothed'. They ate plants with their sharp horn-lined beaks. Then they ground the food in their jaws. The dicynodont was preyed upon by the first sabre-toothed tigers, which were called gorgonopsians (GOR-gon-OP-see-ans). Scientists used to think dicynodont died out at the end of the Triassic period, but the dicynodont found in Australia may have lived alongside the dinosaurs.

 FACT **OR** **FICTION**

Freaky Fact or Fiction

147

In Cretaceous times (144 million to 65 million years ago), an inland sea stretched from north to south through North America. This is called the Western Interior Seaway. Present-day fossilised dinosaur footprints show that the animals travelled along the seaway to Alaska. Some large polar dinosaurs were capable of migrating for distances up to 2600 km (1616 mi).

 FACT **OR** **FICTION**

148

The dinosaur with the longest neck was *Mamenchisaurus* (ma-MEN-chih-SAWR-us). Its neck was almost as long as the rest of its body, with the neck being 11 m (36 ft) of the total 25 m (82 ft) length. This one dinosaur neck was about the length of two Asian elephants in a row! *Mamenchisaurus* was an eating machine. It is thought that it stood in one place and ate everything around it, for as far as its neck would stretch – which was quite a distance. Then it would take another massive step and start eating again. *Mamenchisaurus* lived over 150 million years ago.

✓ **FACT**   **OR**   **FICTION**

149

Famous dinosaur hunter Don Duckett and his wife Daisy were on the Titanic when it sunk in 1912. The Ducketts clung to a piece of wreckage for nearly an hour and were on the point of death. They were saved when a young naval officer named Lee saw them and dragged them aboard a rescue ship. Many years later, Don Duckett repaid the favour. When he discovered a new genus of tyrannosaur (tie-RAN-uh-SAWR) in the Grand Canyon area, he named it the *Gladleesawrus* (GLAD-lee-SAWR-us.)

✓ **FACT** **OR** **FICTION**

150

In 1914, the residents of the small New Zealand town of Kaikoura found something very strange. The entire length of the beach was covered in fossilised dinosaur bones. Overnight there had been a massive underwater earthquake that had shaken the bones free from the ocean depths. Over many years, three dinosaurs were pieced together and are now on display in the New Zealand Museum. Kaikoura's local people collected all the small fossilised bones from the beach. As a thank-you, they were given the honour of naming the new dinosaur genus. They called it *Macropainintheneckasaurus* (MAC-row-PAIN-in-the-NECK-uh-SAWR-us).

✓ **FACT** **OR** **FICTION**

Freaky Fact or Fiction

151

The smallest dinosaur ever found was a fossilised skeleton of a *Mussaurus* (MOOSE-sawr-us). It was 20 cm (8 in) long, a little longer than a human adult's hand. *Mussaurus* lived in desert lands in South America, and its name means 'mouse lizard'. It hatched from tiny eggs 2.5 cm (1 in) long. It is estimated that it would have grown to 3 m (10 ft) long and weighed about 120 kg (260 lb).

 ✓ FACT OR FICTION

152

The Triassic period (248 to 208 million years ago) was when dinosaurs originated. It was a time of dry-climate plants and many reptiles. One of the first true flying reptiles of this time was the pterosaur (TER-uh-SAWR) called *Eudimorphodon* (YOU-die-MOR-fo-don). Found in northern Italy, it had a wingspan of about 1 m (about 3.3 ft) and lived on fish. It had a long tail with a rudder that it used for steering. Paleontologists believe that it was able to flap its wings.

✓ **FACT** **OR** **FICTION**

153

Parasaurolophus (par-a-SAWR-OL-uh-fus) had a most unusual head. Extending out from its skull was a long, tubular growth, or crest. It curved back from its snout for about 1.8 m (6 ft). It seems to have been longer in males than females and had four tubes inside it. This crest may have been used as a signal to let Parasaurolophus recognise one another, or to produce a sound similar to a foghorn. This animal grew to 12 m (40 ft) long and about 2.8 m (9 ft) tall at the hips. Its name means 'crested lizard'.

✓ FACT OR FICTION

154

Some medical students in the US have studied dinosaurs to help them learn about treating humans. In 2006, trainee doctors worked with paleontologists to identify a cancerous growth in a *Camptosaurus* (CAMP-tuh-SAWR-us). They used modern medical technology such as CT scans – advanced tests that use X-rays – to locate the baseball-sized tumour. The students are never likely to forget this kind of cancer again, after finding it in a dinosaur that was about 150 million years old. The University of Pittsburgh School of Medicine and Carnegie Museum of Natural History worked in partnership on the project.

 ✓ **FACT** **OR** **FICTION**

Freaky Fact or Fiction

155

If you want to know what dinosaur ancestors would have looked like, a good example is *Herrerasaurus* (her-RAIR-uh-SAWR-us). It was a two-legged carnivore from Argentina, South America, which lived in the Late Triassic period, about 230 million years ago. It is estimated to have grown to about 3 to 4 m (10 to 13 ft). Its body shape suggests that it was a fast and dangerous predator, with sharp teeth and three-fingered hands. *Herrerasaurus* was named after a rancher, Victorino Herrera, who discovered it in 1958.

 ✓ **FACT** **OR** **FICTION**

156 esearchers at the Australian Dinosaurium have found two dinosaurs that were allergic to each other. Studies have shown that *Ickysaurus* (ICK-ee-SAWR-us) made *Barfasaurus* (BARF-uh-SAWR-us) physically sick. But that did not stop them liking each other. 'We have found that these two animals were inseparable,' said head researcher Dr Preston Starched. 'The constant sickness killed off *Barfasaurus*. We suspect that *Ickysaurus* simply pined away from loneliness. You could say they died for love.'

✓ **FACT** **OR** **FICTION**

Freaky Fact or Fiction

157

One of the most spectacular-looking dinosaurs of all was *Amargasaurus* (ah-MAHR-gah-SAWR-us). We all know that dragons never lived, but if they had, they might have looked like this creature. It had a double row of spines that ran from its neck, all along its back and halfway along its tail. It is named after La Amarga, a canyon in Argentina, where it was found in 1984. This huge herbivore grew to 10 m (33 ft) long and weighed about 5000 kg (11,000 lb).

 ✓ FACT OR FICTION

158

The biggest dinosaur-hunting trip of all took place in Africa in the early 1900s. It began when an engineer, searching for minerals in Tanzania, found pieces of gigantic fossil bones on the surface of the ground. An expedition, led by German scientists, employed over a thousand workers from 1909 to 1911. They dug up nearly 100 skeletons and hundreds of individual bones on a 3 km (1.8 mi) site. As many as 4300 loads of fossilised dinosaur bones were shipped out.

✓ **FACT** **OR** **FICTION**

159

The scientific world was agog in late 2010 with the discovery of a startling new Australian dinosaur called *Backpackasaur* (BAK-pak-uh-sawr). The 74-million-year-old female dinosaur may be the earliest form of kangaroo. It is about the same size as a kangaroo, and it was also a hopper. Unlike the roo, the dinosaur had not one pouch, but two – one in front of its body, and one at the back. The front pouch was most likely used as a place to store food, while its young were carried in the back pouch.

✓ **FACT** **OR** **FICTION**

160

Can you imagine a watch made out of dinosaur poop? In 2010, Swiss watchmaker Artya and designer Yvan Arpa created such a watch. The fossilised dung used in the watch's creation came from a plant-eating dinosaur that lived in North America 100 million years ago.

The watch is self-winding and has a sapphire coating. It is water resistant and comes with a two-year warranty. Its strap is fashioned out of American cane toad skin. It is valued at US$11,290 (A$13,370 or £7715). It's not every day you can buy a watch made from fossilised dinosaur poop, right?

 ✓ **FACT** **OR** **FICTION**

Freaky Fact or Fiction

161 Most dinosaur footprints have three toes. The other two toes were held high off the ground. Or they were lost during evolution. Tracks can provide helpful information about the behaviour of dinosaurs. The shape of a footprint shows which kind of dinosaur it was and how large it was. The space between the prints shows how fast it was moving. Multiple tracks show that a herd passed by.

✓ FACT OR FICTION

162

Mary Anning (1799–1847) was an early pioneer of fossil collecting. She lived all her life in Lyme Regis on the Dorset coast in England. The sea cliffs there are one of the world's most renowned places for early Jurassic marine reptile fossils. When she was only 11, Mary found her first important specimen – the whole skeleton of a large ichthyosaur (IK-thee-uh-sawr). Mary and her brother Joseph were encouraged by their father to find fossils as he then sold them to people as curiosities. Mary found the first complete plesiosaur (PLEE-see-uh-sawr) skeleton and the first British pterosaur (TER-uh-SAWR).

✓ **FACT** **OR** **FICTION**

Freaky Fact or Fiction

163

The author of the novel *Jurassic Park* (from which the famous movie was made) had a dinosaur named after him. The author is Michael Crichton and the dinosaur is *Crichtonsaurus* (CRY-ton-SAWR-us). This plant-eater lived about 90 to 95 million years ago. It was a low-slung, medium-sized armoured dinosaur that lived in Asia during the Middle Cretaceous period.

 ✓ **FACT**   **OR**   **FICTION**

164

In 1993, *Attenborosaurus* (AT-ten-bur-row-SAWR-us) was named after the British natural history filmmaker Sir David Attenborough. *Attenborosaurus* was an aquatic reptile with a very large head and short neck. A pliosaur (PLY-uh-sawr), *Attenborosaurus* had only a few massive teeth. It is thought it used these to eat fish during the Early Jurassic period. The original fossil of *Attenborosaurus* was destroyed in a bombing raid on England during World War II. Luckily, a plaster cast had been made.

✓ **FACT** **OR** **FICTION**

Freaky Fact or Fiction

165

Did you know that there is a dinosaur named after a family of famous writers? The Brontë sisters – Charlotte, Emily and Anne – all died at a young age, but not before they had written novels that eventually made them famous. In 1895, a new genus of dinosaur was found in West Yorkshire, not far from where the sisters had lived. To honour their memory, the dinosaur was called the Brontësaurus (BRON-tee-SAWR-us). This dinosaur is not related to *Brontosaurus* (BRON-toe-SAWR-us).

 ✓ **FACT**   **OR**   **FICTION**

166

When it was first found in the Antarctic, *Cryolophosaurus* (CRY-oh-LOAF-oh-SAWR-us) was nicknamed Elvisaurus, after the singer Elvis Presley. This was because it had a horizontal crest on top of its head that was similar to Presley's hairstyle. About 6.1 m (20 ft) long, *Cryolophosaurus* lived in the Early Jurassic period. At that time, Antarctica was not the freezing place it is today, so *Cryolophosaurus* did not need fur or feathers to keep it warm.

 FACT **OR** **FICTION**

167

Itchyosaur (IT-chee-uh-sawr) is so named because it spent much of its life itching. Cellular examination of this animal's skeleton proved that its hide was infested with dandruff. Its only relief would have been to plunge into the sea and have a good long wash, but as it couldn't swim, this often proved a bad idea.

✓ **FACT** **OR** **FICTION**

168 *C*olepiocephale (co-LEE-pee-oh-SEF-ah-lee) was given a funny name. *Colepio* is the Greek root for 'knuckle' and *cephale* means 'head'. Put them together and what have you got? That's right – a dinosaur named Knucklehead! A two-legged herbivore, this dinosaur was small – about 90 cm (3 ft) long. It was a type of pachycephalosaur (PACK-ee-SEF-uh-lo-sawr) or thick-headed lizard. As the name suggests, these dinosaurs had a lot of bone on top of their heads. This probably came in handy to head-butt rivals.

✓ **FACT** **OR** **FICTION**

Freaky Fact or Fiction

169

Bambiraptor (BAM-bee-RAP-tor) sounds like it's a character from a Disney movie. But it is the real name of a dinosaur that was found by a 14-year-old boy in 1995. The boy found the near-complete skeleton of *Bambiraptor* in Montana's Glacier National Park, USA. This tiny, two-legged, bird-like raptor may have been covered with feathers. Its brain was almost as big as that of modern birds. Paleontologists study *Bambiraptor* to work out the evolutionary link between ancient dinosaurs and modern birds. And yes, it was named after the Disney Bambi character!

 FACT **OR** **FICTION**

170

Shuvuuia (shoe-VOO-yee-ah) is a prehistoric animal that paleontologists can't quite figure out. Was it a dinosaur or a bird? It had a small, bird-like head but dinosaur-like forelimbs with long legs and three-toed feet. It was found in Mongolia and its name is taken from the Mongolian word for 'bird'. It was about as big as a chicken and was a quick mover that probably fed on insects and worms. It's not quite as scary as some of its more famous cousins, but it shows that dinosaurs came in all shapes and sizes.

✓ FACT OR FICTION

Freaky Fact or Fiction

171

As its name suggests, *Supersaurus* (SOO-per-SAWR-us) was a massive dinosaur. It was probably as long as half a football field. However, it wasn't called *Supersaurus* just because of its size. This dinosaur could fly at great speeds, although only for short distances. As well, its armour-plated body could easily have withstood bullets. Unlike Superman, it did not have X-ray vision. In fact, it was short-sighted. But it made up for this by having quadraphonic hearing. That is, it could hear from four directions at once. This was indeed a super dinosaur.

 ✓ **FACT** **OR** **FICTION**

172 *U**tahraptor* (YOO-tah-RAP-tor) was probably one of the best-equipped killing machines of all dinosaurs. In 1991, a well-preserved skeleton was found in Utah, USA. *Utahraptor* was a carnivore with large eyes, long hands and strong, clawed feet. Its main weapons were the hooked claws on its feet. While its 20-cm (8-in) claws struck out, it balanced on its tail. With this method it was a serious fighter that could kill animals much larger than itself.

✓ **FACT** **OR** **FICTION**

Freaky Fact or Fiction

173

Researchers at the George Washington Dinosaur Centre have found evidence of a highly intelligent dinosaur. It was a rough-necked megabore (MEG-uh-BAWR) called *Bragasaurus* (BRAG-uh-SAWR-us). Deep-heat analysis of soil and bone samples proved that this reptile was a clever mimic. Head researcher Dr Allie Baba explained, '*Bragasaurus* could imitate other animals – not just frogs and birds, but maybe cockroaches, too. We still don't know why it did it, but we suspect it just liked to show off.'

✓ FACT OR FICTION

174

When he made the movie *Jurassic Park* in 1993, director Steven Spielberg perhaps did more than anyone to get people interested in dinosaurs. One of those whose fame and reputation grew because of the movie was *Velociraptor* (vel-os-i-RAP-tor). However, although they were referred to as *Velociraptor* in the movie, the dinosaurs shown were actually the much larger and more fearsome *Deinonchysus* (dye-NON-i-kus).

✓ **FACT** **OR** **FICTION**

Freaky Fact or Fiction

175

One day in 1852, Ernest Fallow set off to buy an engagement ring for his girlfriend Polly. Next to the jewellery shop a very special auction was taking place. The highest bidder would win the naming rights for a new dinosaur genus. Fallow bid all the money that he had, and soon the naming rights were his. Polly was not impressed that he had named a dinosaur *Pollysaurus* (POLL-ee-SAWR-us), instead of buying a ring. It only made things worse when Ernest explained that he had done it because the dinosaur reminded him of her. Their marriage did not take place.

 FACT **OR** **FICTION**

Dinosaurs

176

The Australian airline Qantas has a dinosaur named after it – but it couldn't fly. *Qantassaurus* (KWAN-tuh-SAWR-us), which lived over 100 million years ago, was about the size of a small kangaroo but it is not thought to have been a hopping animal. Discovered in 1996, it was a herbivore that was unique to Australia. It was named after Qantas to honour the company for its work in transporting dinosaur exhibitions.

 ✓ **FACT** **OR** **FICTION**

Freaky Fact or Fiction

177 **A** new device called a Brain Gauge can tell how smart dinosaurs were. Scientists say *Troödon* (TRO-uh-don) was the smartest dinosaur. It had its own primitive language. This was only a series of grunts, but it made enough sense for *Troödons* to have conversations. It also had very basic counting skills, but was probably hopeless at long division. The least smart dinosaur was *Derrosaurus* (DERR-o-SAWR-us). Its extinction was due to the fact that it kept eating its tail. It thought it was being followed.

 ✓ **FACT** **OR** **FICTION**

178

Australian scientists have discovered a dinosaur that is an ancient relative of the kangaroo. It was discovered in 2002 by an opal miner in South Australia. The dinosaur is about three times the size of a kangaroo. In all other aspects the two animals are very similar. The dinosaur even had a pouch to carry its young. It is called *Skippysaurus* (SKIPP-ee-SAWR-us).

✓ **FACT** **OR** **FICTION**

Freaky Fact or Fiction

179 A bone bed discovered in Zhucheng, China in 2009 could be the last place dinosaurs gathered before their extinction. Some 15,000 bones were found stacked on top of each other at the site, which is thought to be the world's largest bone bed. Scientists say the bones date to the end of the Cretaceous period, which was the time that dinosaur extinction occurred. It is unknown yet why the dinosaurs came to this place to die.

 ✓ **FACT** **OR** **FICTION**

180 In 2010, a team of international researchers made a dramatic breakthrough. While studying fossils of the oldest known 'dinobird' *Archaeopteryx* (ahr-kee-OP-ter-iks), they found chemical remains of the animal itself. Previously it was thought that the fossils were just impressions of organic material that had long ago decomposed. Powerful X-rays revealed that the fossils held fragments of actual feathers. They contained the same elements that are found in the feathers of modern-day birds. Researcher Bob Morton said, 'The discovery that certain fossils retain the chemistry of the original organisms offers scientists a new avenue for learning about long-extinct creatures.'

✓ **FACT**   **OR**   **FICTION**

Freaky Fact or Fiction

181

As a group, it is estimated that dinosaurs lived for over 160 million years. But how long did individual dinosaurs live? When the first studies on ageing were made, it was thought that dinosaurs may have lived hundreds of years. However, with new techniques come new estimates. Now scientists say that the large herbivores may have lived for about 80 years, give or take a few. Smaller, carnivorous specimens probably lived for 20 to 30 years. So it seems that eating your greens is pretty good for you.

✓ FACT OR FICTION

182

The fossil remains of *Explorasaurus* (ex-PLORE-uh-SAWR-us) have been found in every country of the world. It is the most travelled of all the dinosaurs. Scientists can only guess the reasons for this. Some say it was curious and liked to see what was over the next hill. Others say it was restless, forever looking for some new adventure. And there are those who believe the dinosaur simply had a poor sense of direction and was always getting lost.

✓ **FACT** **OR** **FICTION**

183

Dinosaur eggs were once found under the New York subway. The eggs were discovered in late 1948 by a man named John Doe. He immediately rang the New York Zoo to report the find. In the meantime, his wife, Jane Doe, had cooked the eggs for breakfast, and eaten them. She immediately became ill. A doctor was quickly on the scene but, unfortunately, Mrs Doe's life was pronounced extinct.

 ✓ **FACT** **OR** **FICTION**

184

A paleontologist named Earl Douglass first discovered dinosaur fossils in Utah, USA, in 1909. He went on to find thousands more and the region he worked in became Dinosaur National Monument. Today, examples of more than half of North America's dinosaurs from the Jurassic period can be found in the park's Dinosaur National Monument Quarry. A new species of dinosaur named *Abydosaurus mcintoshi* (a-BID-oh-SAWR-us MAK-in-tosh-ee) was found in the park in 2010. *Abydosaurus* was from the sauropod (SAWR-uh-pod) family, which were huge herbivores. A dig team, who used explosives to reach the specimens, found four skulls, and two of them were intact.

✓ **FACT** **OR** **FICTION**

185

Epidendrosaurus (EP-ih-DEN-droh-SAWR-us) was one of the earliest 'dinobirds'. No-one knows for sure if it flew, though it's doubtful. Nevertheless, it is thought that it lived in trees and had feathers. It also had something in common with a present-day animal called the aye-aye. These rare creatures are lemurs that are only found in Madagascar. Like *Epidendrosaurus*, the aye-aye has one very long finger on each hand to allow it to dig for grubs and insects in holes and tree bark. It's very likely that this is what *Epidendrosaurus* did as well.

✓ **FACT** **OR** **FICTION**

186

Carnotaurus (KAR-no-TAWR-us) was an odd-looking dinosaur from South America. It had a small skull for such a big animal, and it also had tiny arms. Its name means 'meat-eating bull', so if you guessed that it was a carnivore that looked a bit like a bull, you were right. It is best known because it had bull-like horns above each eye. It was around 7.6 m (25 ft) long and weighed about 1 t (1.1 US ton).

 FACT **OR** **FICTION**

Freaky Fact or Fiction

187

The first dinosaur skeleton ever to be put together was truly a jigsaw. For nearly 200 years the credit for assembling the dinosaur has been given to famed dinosaur hunter Lord Claude Broad. Now, with the release of his lost journal, the truth has finally been revealed. Lord Broad invited the members of the Surrey Jigsaw Club over for tea. Afterwards, he challenged them to the ultimate jigsaw puzzle. The members took just two days to connect more than 40,000 pieces of fossilised dinosaur bones.

 ✓ FACT OR FICTION

188

If you look at the skeleton of a *Tuojiangosaurus* (too-HWANG-oh-SAWR-us) you might just start to believe in dragons. The partial remains of two of these dragon look-alikes have been found in Sichuan Province, China. Records show that many hundreds of years ago villagers collected fossils from here and sold them as dragon bones. These were highly prized for use in traditional medicine. *Tuojiangosaurus* was a prickly customer. It had large spikes over most of its body, including its tail and shoulders. It was a herbivore that was about 7 m (23 ft) long. Its name means 'Tuo River lizard'.

✓ **FACT** **OR** **FICTION**

Freaky Fact or Fiction

189

It is clear that dinosaurs migrated in vast numbers. Across western North America massive 'bone beds' of several species have been found. These dinosaur graveyards can hold the remains of hundreds or thousands of beasts. It makes sense that herds of this size couldn't stay in the same place for too long, because they would soon exhaust food supplies. They had to keep moving.

✓ **FACT** **OR** **FICTION**

190

In 2010, a yoga instructor in Argentina found herself in an amazing position. While performing her exercises she accidentally came across some very big footprints. Scientists found that the tracks, which were in good condition and up to 1.2 m (4 ft) in diameter, had been made more than 90 million years ago by sauropod (SAWR-uh-pod) dinosaurs. The find was in an area that is known as Argentina's Jurassic Park. In 1993, the remains of a *Giganotosaurus* (JI-ga-NO-to-SAWR-us), the largest carnivorous dinosaur in the world, were found there.

✓ **FACT**   **OR**   **FICTION**

Freaky Fact or Fiction

191 In 2009, US scientists discovered one of the world's largest dinosaur 'graveyards'. In a paper released by the Boston Academy of Advanced Dinosauria (BAAD), it is revealed that close to one million dinosaurs died at the site in Nevada. One of the most interesting features of the site is that large boulders found nearby were actually made of coprolite, or petrified dinosaur dung. Incredibly, when the outer layer of the boulders was chipped away, the smell of the dung was still strong.

✓ FACT OR FICTION

192 In 1995, while studying meteorites that had fallen in Arizona, a research team found minute evidence of dinosaur fossils. Professor Miriam Crock, head researcher at the New York Meteorium, said that it is 'highly unlikely' that the find could mean dinosaurs once existed on other planets. 'There is no doubt that the particles we detected came from a *stegosaur* (STEG-uh-SAWR),' she said. 'However, as scientists, we believe there has to be a logical reason for this. It could be that some freak atmospheric condition caused the fossil tissue to be embedded in a meteorite.'

✓ **FACT** **OR** **FICTION**

193

Sometimes just one surviving fossil is all there is to show for a whole species of dinosaur. This is the case with *Eustreptospondylus oxoniensis* (yoo-strep-toe-SPON-die-lus OX-on-ee-EN-sis). The one and only specimen was found in a quarry in Oxford, England, and was named by Richard Owen, the man who first coined the name 'dinosaur'. The specimen was originally about 5 m (16.4 ft) long and weighed 500 kg (1102 lb); however, it was probably a young dinosaur that was still growing.

 ✓ **FACT**   **OR**   **FICTION**

Dinosaurs

It seems that dinosaurs may have been the first lovers of fast food. With their very long necks, herbivores were able to stand in one place and simply swivel their necks about to find what was on the plant menu. Researchers from the University of Bonn in Germany, led by Professor Martin Sander, have found that dinosaurs gulped their food instead of chewing it. Chewing takes time. An animal as large as a dinosaur needed to eat quickly in order to maintain its energy demands. Professor Sander said this explained why dinosaurs grew to be so large.

 FACT   **OR**   **FICTION**

Freaky Fact or Fiction

195 A dog named Blinky once 'killed' a *Tyrannosaurus rex* (tie-RAN-uh-SAWR-us rex). In 1986, Blinky broke away from its owner while out walking in London's Hyde Park. The dog kept running until it reached the Queen Victoria Dinosaur Museum. Slipping through a back door, he found himself surrounded by towering dinosaurs. Blinky loved bones, so he just had to have one. Before security guards could stop him, he dived on a *T. rex* and pulled a thigh bone free. The *T. rex* collapsed into a million broken pieces. Blinky is now in the record books as the only dog to destroy a dinosaur.

 FACT **OR** **FICTION**

196 **T**orosaurus (TOR-uh-SAWR-us) was discovered in North America in 1891. It is not named after a bull, as the prefix *toro* suggests. Its name means 'pierced lizard'. It was called this because it has large holes in its skull. A herbivore, it had a very large frill, or skull plate, and two fearsome horns. *Torosaurus* probably reached a length of 7.5 m (25 ft) and weighed about 3.6 t (4 US t). It was long considered to be related to *Triceratops* (try-SAIR-a-tops) but in 2010 the discovery was made that *Triceratops* is just a juvenile *Torosaurus*! So, the *Torosaurus* became extinct for a second time when it was reclassified.

 FACT **OR** **FICTION**

Freaky Fact or Fiction

197

In 1972, a science teacher named Al Lakusta went on a picnic at Pipestone Creek, in Alberta, Canada. He noticed something that looked like brown fossilised rib fragments. Mr Lakusta had stumbled on one of the world's richest dinosaur bone beds. As large as a football field and more than 70 million years old, it was the last resting place of a rare dinosaur, which was partly named in the teacher's honour. It is called *Pachyrhinosaurus lakustai* (PAK-ee-rye-no-SAWR-us la-KUS-tye). By 2010, more than a dozen skulls had been taken from the site. There is still much more excavation to be done.

 FACT **OR** **FICTION**

198

Scientists have put together a theory about the origin of massive dinosaur bone beds, such as the one in Pipestone Creek, Canada. They say it is likely that herds of migrating dinosaurs were crossing a flooding river, when many of them were swept away and killed. Scavenger dinosaurs picked up the smell of the rotting carcasses and went into the river, only to die themselves. This pattern continued, creating huge bone beds.

 FACT OR **FICTION**

Freaky Fact or Fiction

199

New studies show that dinosaur soup could hold the secret to weight loss. The bones are crushed and deep-frozen before being made into a soup. British woman Twiggy Reed says she lost half her body weight after going on the dinosaur diet. 'When you eat something that's millions of years old you usually expect it will be kind of stale,' she said. 'But it wasn't. Just add a little salt and pepper and it's lovely.'

✓ FACT OR FICTION

200

Tyler Lyson was 16 when he found his mummy. No, not his mother, his dinosaur mummy! In 1999, Lyson found a huge herbivore called *Edmontosaurus* (ed-MON-tuh-SAWR-us). Not only bones, but also fossilised skin, ligaments and tendons were identified. Nicknamed Dakota, because it was found in the US state of North Dakota, the dinosaur is said to be one of the best-preserved dinosaurs ever found. In fact, one leading scientist has stated it may be the closest we'll ever come to seeing a living dinosaur.

✓ **FACT** **OR** **FICTION**

201 Scientists are confident that one day dinosaurs will live again. Professor Matt Hari of Japan's Dinosaur Institute said the technology was already in place for bringing back the ancient reptile. 'All we need is more DNA,' he said. 'At present our vats are about a third full. Each time a dinosaur is found we get a little more. My guess is that in 10 to 20 years the dinosaur will be back.'

 ✓ **FACT** **OR** **FICTION**

202

When a new discovery of a dinosaur is made it is very much like finding a needle in a haystack. After all, they have been extinct for 65 million years. Over 700 species of dinosaur have been named so far. It is estimated that at least this many again are still out there, waiting to be found. But this is a very small figure when compared to other creatures. For instance, there are about 10,000 known bird species, 20,000 fish species and as for insects, well, there are a lot. Estimates range from 1.5 million to 30 million.

✓ **FACT** **OR** **FICTION**

Freaky Fact or Fiction

203

Psittacosaurus (SIT-uh-ko-SAWR-us) was on the small side for a dinosaur. When it stood up on its back legs it was still only about 1.2 m (4 ft) tall. It was roughly 2 m (6.5 ft) long. Its odd name means 'parrot lizard'. That's because its head resembled a parrot's. A herbivore and probably a fast mover, it has been found in China, Mongolia and Thailand. Scientists think that, like the parrot, this dinosaur ate seeds and nuts, and most likely cracked the nuts with its tough beak.

 FACT **OR** **FICTION**

Dinosaurs

204

The dinosaur called *Styrocosaurus* (sty-ROW-kuh-SAWR-us) could best be described as a very odd mix. It had several long horns jutting out above its frill. On its snout was another horn, very similar to that of the present-day rhinoceros. And, like *Psittacosaurus* (SIT-uh-ko-SAWR-us), its snout was shaped like a parrot's beak. A herbivore, it was about as tall as a rhino and grew to about 5.2 m (17 ft) long. It could weigh as much as 2.7 t (3 US t).

 FACT **OR** **FICTION**

Answers

1. Fact.

2. Fact.

3. Fact.

4. Fact.

5. Fact.

6. Fact.

7. **Fiction.**

8. Fact.

9. Fact.

10. Fact.

11. **Fiction.**

12. Fact.

13. **Fiction**, but you may have heard of a dog breed called the golden retriever.

14. **Fiction.**

15. Fact.

16. Fact.

17. Fact.

18. **Fiction.**

19. Fact.

20. Fact.

21. Fact.

22. Fact.

23. **Fiction.**

24. Fact.

25. Fact.

26. Fact.

27. Fact.

28. **Fiction.**

29. Fact.

30. Fact.

31. **Fiction.**

32. Fact.

33. Fact.

34. **Fiction.**

35. Fact.

36. Fact.

37. **Fiction.**

38. Fact.

39. Fact.

40. Fact.

41. Fact.

42. Fiction.

43. Fact.

44. Fact.

45. Fact.

46. Fiction, but Elvis Presley was born in Tupelo, Mississippi.

47. Fact.

48. Fact.

49. Fact.

50. Fact.

51. Fiction. *Dollodon* was really a dinosaur, but it was not made into a toy, nor did the Transylvanians name it.

52. Fact.

53. Fact.

54. Fact.

55. Fact.

56. Fiction. *Afrovenator* was a dinosaur, but was not named after an African inventor.

57. Fact.

58. Fact.

59. Fact.

60. Fiction. All information here is fictional. However, there was a dinosaur with a similar name, the *Chungkingosaurus*.

61. Fact.

62. Fact.

63. Fact.

64. Fact.

65. Fact.

66. Fact.

67. Fact.

68. Fiction, but there is a dinosaur called Bambiraptor.

69. Fact.

Answers

70. Fact.

71. Fact.

72. Fact.

73. Fact.

74. Fiction.

75. Fact.

76. Fact.

77. Fiction. *El Dorado* is the name of a legendary lost city of gold. Dinosaurs are not part of the legend. However, there were gold rushes in the Klondike and Yukon, and *El Dorado* does mean 'the golden one' in Spanish.

78. Fact.

79. Fact.

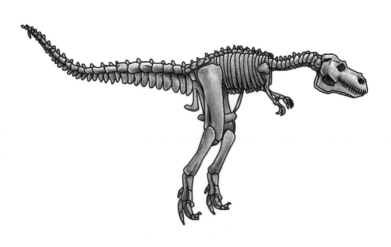

80. Fact.

81. Fact.

82. Fiction.

83. Fiction.

84. Fiction.

85. Fact.

86. Fact.

87. Fact.

88. Fact.

89. Fiction.

90. Fact.

91. Fact.

92. Fact.

93. Fact.

94. Fiction, although there is evidence that dinosaurs were migratory animals.

95. Fiction. Please note that Horace Rubble is no relation to Barney Rubble, best friend of Fred Flintstone, from the movie and television show *The Flintstones*.

96. Fact.

97. Fact.

98. Fact.

99. Fact.

100. Fiction.

101. Fact.

102. Fact.

103. Fact.

104. Fiction.

105. Fact.

106. Fact.

107. Fact.

108. Fiction.

109. Fact.

110. Fact.

111. Fact.

112. Fact.

113. Fact.

114. Fiction.

115. Fact.

Answers

● ● ● ● ● ● ● ● ● ● ● ● ● ● ● ● ● ● ● ●

116. Fact.

117. Fact.

118. Fact.

119. Fiction, and there are no polar bears at the South Pole.

120. Fact.

121. Fact.

122. Fact.

123. Fact.

124. Fact.

125. Fiction.

126. Fact.

127. Fiction.

128. Fact.

129. Fact.

130. Fact.

131. Fact.

132. Fact.

133. Fiction.

134. Fact.

135. Fact.

136. Fact.

137. Fact.

138. Fact.

139. Fiction. Though a Queensland schoolboy did find ichthyosaur remains while working in a school vegetable patch in 2010, there was no library book.

140. Fiction, but Samuel Johnson did write one of the first dictionaries.

141. Fact.

142. Fact.

143. Fact.

144. Fiction.

145. Fact.

146. Fact.

147. Fact.

148. Fact.

149. Fiction.

150. Fiction.

151. Fact.

152. Fact.

153. Fact.

154. Fact.

155. Fact.

156. Fiction.

157. Fact.

158. Fact.

159. Fiction.

160. Fact.

161. Fact.

162. Fact.

163. Fact.

164. Fact.

165. Fiction, but the Brontës were famous writers.

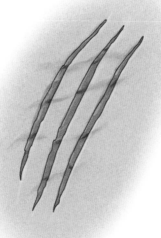

Answers

166. Fact.

167. Fiction. However, ichthyosaurs are marine reptiles from the time of the dinosaurs that have a similar name.

168. Fact.

169. Fact.

170. Fact.

171. Fiction. Though there is a dinosaur called *Supersaurus,* it didn't have super powers.

172. Fact.

173. Fiction.

174. Fact.

175. Fiction.

176. Fact.

177. Fiction, but *Troödon* is considered to have been the smartest dinosaur.

178. Fiction.

179. Fact.

180. Fact.

181. Fact.

182. Fiction.

183. Fiction.

184. Fact.

185. Fact.

186. Fact.

187. Fiction.

188. Fact.

189. Fact.

190. Fact.

191. Fiction. However, some fossilised dung does still smell after thousands of years. One such case is the giant ground sloth from North America; it was dead 15,000 years, but was still smelly!

192. Fiction.

193. Fact.

194. Fact.

Sources

1. Michael Benton, *The Penguin Historical Atlas of the Dinosaurs*, 1996

2. Michael Benton, *The Penguin Historical Atlas of the Dinosaurs*, 1996; US Geological Survey, http://pubs.usgs.gov, 2001; Encyclopaedia Britannica Online, www.britannica.com, 2010

3. Michael Benton, *The Penguin Historical Atlas of the Dinosaurs*, 1996; US Geological Survey, http://pubs.usgs.gov, 2001; Encyclopaedia Britannica Online, www.britannica.com, 2010

4. Michael Benton, *Kingfisher Factfinder: Dinosaurs* (book), 2001; Natural History Museum, www.nhm.ac.uk, 2010; Encyclopaedia Britannica Online, www.britannica.com, 2010

5. *Guinness World Records 2009* (book), 2009

6. *Guinness World Records 2009* (book), 2009

7. Fiction.

8. *Scholastic Australian & World Records 2009* (book), 2009

9. 'Mystery Solved! Giant Asteroid Killed the Dinosaurs, say Scientists', NYDailyNews.com, www.nydailynews.com, 2010

10. Encyclopædia Britannica Online, www.britannica.com, 2010

11. Fiction.

12. Enchanted Learning, www.enchantedlearning.com, 2010

13. Fiction.

14. Fiction.

15. Michael Benton, *Kingfisher Factfinder: Dinosaurs* (book), 2001; Answers.com: ReferenceAnswers, www.answers.com, 2010; Enchanted Learning, www.enchantedlearning.com, 2010

16. Stanford University News Services, http://news.stanford.edu, 1996; Enchanted Learning, www.enchantedlearning.com, 2010

17. '10 Facts About Tyrannosaurus Rex', Bob Strauss, About.com, http://dinosaurs.about.com, 2010

18. Fiction.

19. Brian Cooley and Mary Ann Wilson, *Make-A-Saurus: My Life with Raptors and Other Dinosaurs* (book), 2000; David Norman and Angela Milner, *Collins Eyewitness Guides: Dinosaurs* (book), 1991; Benjamin Waterhouse Hawkins, www.bwaterhousehawkins.com

20. AgeofDinosaurs.com, http://ageofdinosaurs.com; Scott Hocknull and Dr Alex Cook, *Amazing Facts about Australian Dinosaurs* (book), 2006

21. Michael Benton, *Kingfisher Factfinder: Dinosaurs* (book), 2001; Oceans of Kansas Paleontology, www.oceansofkansas.com, 2009

22. Michael Benton, *Kingfisher Factfinder: Dinosaurs* (book), 2001; Michael Benton, *The Penguin Historical Atlas of the Dinosaurs*, 1996; Gondwana Studios, www.gondwanastudios.com, 2010

23. Fiction.

24. Australian Museum, http://australianmuseum.net.au, 2009; Enchanted Learning, www.enchantedlearning.com, 2010; Dinosaurs for Kids, www.kidsdinos.com, 2010; AgeofDinosaurs.com, http://ageofdinosaurs.com

25. Enchanted Learning, www.enchantedlearning.com, 2010; Dinosaurs for Kids, www.kidsdinos.com, 2010

26. Michael Benton, *Kingfisher Factfinder: Dinosaurs* (book), 2001; Michael Benton, *The Penguin Historical Atlas of the Dinosaurs*, 1996; Strange Science, www.strangescience.net.htm, 2009

27. Michael Benton, *Kingfisher Factfinder: Dinosaurs* (book), 2001; Encyclopaedia Britannica Online, www.britannica.com, 2010

28. Fiction.

29. ABC News, Australia, www.abc.net.au, 2007; Cosmos, www.cosmosmagazine.com, 2007; The Hairy Museum of Natural History, www.hmnh.org, 2008

30. Enchanted Learning, www.enchantedlearning.com, 2010; HowStuffWorks.com, http://animals.howstuffworks.com, 2008; Michael Benton, *Kingfisher Factfinder: Dinosaurs* (book), 2001

31. Fiction.

32. Enchanted Learning, www.enchantedlearning.com, 2010; Dr David Norman, *The Illustrated Encyclopedia of Dinosaurs* (book), 1985; Science Museum of Minnesota: Science Buzz, www.sciencebuzz.org, 2008

33. Michael Benton, *Kingfisher Factfinder: Dinosaurs* (book), 2001; 'Alamosaurus', Bob Strauss, About.com, http://dinosaurs.about.com, 2010; National Park Service, US Department of the Interior, www.nps.gov, 2010

34. Fiction.

35. Michael Benton, *Kingfisher Factfinder: Dinosaurs* (book), 2001; Walking with Dinosaurs (ABC, BBC), http://abc.net.au, 1999; New Mexico Museum of Natural History and Science, http://nmstatefossil.org, 2009

36. HowStuffWorks.com, http://animals.howstuffworks.com, 2010; Dinosaurs for Kids, www.kidsdinos.com, 2010; AgeofDinosaurs.com, http://ageofdinosaurs.com; 'Saichania', Bob Strauss, About.com, http://dinosaurs.about.com, 2010

37. Fiction.

38. Walking with Dinosaurs (ABC, BBC), www.abc.net.au, 1999; Michael Benton, *Kingfisher Factfinder: Dinosaurs* (book), 2001; 'Quetzalcoatlus', Bob Strauss, About.com, http://dinosaurs.about.com, 2010

39. 'Untouched on a Shelf for 113 Years: A Dusty Bone of the Dinosaur No One Knew Existed', Guardian News and Media, www.guardian.co.uk, 2007; Mike Taylor, www.miketaylor.org.uk, 2007

40. Alaska Museum of Natural History, www.alaskamuseum.org, 2005; Encyclopaedia Britannica Online, www.britannica.com, 2010

41. 'The 10 Smartest Dinosaurs', About.com, http://dinosaurs.about.com, 2010

42. Fiction.

43. US Geological Survey, http://pubs.usgs.gov.html, 2001; Geology Shop, www.geologyshop.co.uk, 2002; Life's Little Mysteries, www.lifeslittlemysteries.com, 2010

44. Walking with Dinosaurs (ABC, BBC), www.abc.net.au, 1999; Michael Benton, *Kingfisher Factfinder: Dinosaurs* (book), 2001

45. Australian Age of Dinosaurs, www.aaodl.com, 2009; Queensland Museum, www.qm.qld.gov.au, 2010

46. Fiction.

47. David Norman and Angela Milner, *Collins Eyewitness Guides: Dinosaurs* (book), 1991; Enchanted Learning, www.enchantedlearning.com, 2010

48. Dinosaur Facts, www.dinosaurfact.net, 2010; Paleos: The History of Life on Earth, www.palaeos.com, 2005; National History Museum, www.nhm.ac.uk, 2007

49. Michael Benton, *Kingfisher Factfinder: Dinosaurs* (book), 2001; Enchanted Learning, www.enchantedlearning.com, 2010

50. Michael Benton, *Kingfisher Factfinder: Dinosaurs* (book), 2001; Answers.com, www.answers.com, 2010; 'Dimorphodon', Bob Strauss, About.com, http://dinosaurs.about.com, 2010

51. Fiction.

52. Enchanted Learning, www.enchantedlearning.com, 2010; 'How Dinosaurs Are Named', Bob Strauss, About.com, http://dinosaurs.about.com, 2010

Sources

53. Dinosaur Facts, www.dinosaurfact.net, 2010; 'Chirostenotes', Bob Strauss, About.com, http://dinosaurs.about.com, 2010

54. Enchanted Learning, www.enchantedlearning.com, 2010

55. Museum Victoria, http://museumvictoria.com.au; My Jurassic Park, www.myjurassicpark.com, 2006

56. Fiction.

57. 'True-Color Dinosaur Revealed: First Full-Body Rendering', National Geographic, http://news.nationalgeographic.com, 2010

58. Hooper Virtual Natural History Museum, Ottawa–Carleton Geoscience Centre, http://hoopermuseum.earthsci.carleton.ca, 1998; Enchanted Learning, www.enchantedlearning.com, 2010; 'Dsungaripterus', Bob Strauss, About.com, http://dinosaurs.about.com, 2010

59. Michael Benton, *Kingfisher Factfinder: Dinosaurs* (book), 2001; Benedictine University, www.ben.edu, 2010; HowStuffWorks.com, http://animals.howstuffworks.com, 2010

60. Fiction.

61. Dinosaur Den, www.dinosaurden.co.uk, 2003; 'Dinosaur of the Day – Gargoyleosaurus', Bob Strauss, About.com, http://dinosaurs.about.com, 2009; Enchanted Learning, www.enchantedlearning.com, 2010

62. Encyclopædia Britannica Online, www.britannica.com, 2010; HowStuffWorks.com, http://animals.howstuffworks.com, 2010; Canadian Museum of Nature, http://nature.ca, 2010

63. Dinosaurs for Kids, www.kidsdinos.com, 2010; GEOERA: The World of Dinosaurs, www.dinosaurusi.com; Encyclo: Online Encyclopedia, www.encyclo.co.uk, 2010; AgeofDinosaurs.com, http://ageofdinosaurs.com.htm

64. National History Museum, www.nhm.ac.uk, 2007; 'Telmatosaurus', Bob Strauss, About.com, http://dinosaurs.about.com, 2010; DinoDictionary.com, www.dinodictionary.com, 2005

65. Museum Victoria, http://museumvictoria.com.au

66. Michael Benton, *Kingfisher Factfinder: Dinosaurs* (book), 2001; University of California Museum of Paleontology, www.ucmp.berkeley.edu, 2005

67. 'Digging Up Fossils', Scholastic: Teachers, www2.scholastic.com, 1988

68. Fiction.

69. Enchanted Learning, www.enchantedlearning.com, 2010; 'Zuniceratops', Bob Strauss, About.com, http://dinosaurs.about.com.htm, 2010

70. Children's Museum of Indianapolis, www.childrensmuseum.org, 2010; British Council, LearnEnglish Central, www.britishcouncil.org.htm

71. Australian Museum, http://australianmuseum.net.au, 2009; Museum of Nature & Science Dallas, Texas, www.natureandscience.org, 2010

72. 'Dinosaur Had Crocodile-Like Skull', National Geographic News, http://news.nationalgeographic.com.html, 2008; Michael Benton, *Kingfisher Factfinder: Dinosaurs* (book), 2001; 'Dinosaur directory: Baryonyx', guardian.co.uk, www.guardian.co.uk, 2006

73. 'The First Mammals – Mammals of the Triassic, Jurassic and Cretaceous Periods', Bob Strauss, About.com, http://dinosaurs.about.com, 2010; Weber State University, Utah, http://faculty.weber.edu, 2010

74. Fiction.

75. American Museum of Natural History, www.amnh.org, 2006

76. Michael Benton, *Kingfisher Factfinder: Dinosaurs* (book), 2001; Answers.com: ReferenceAnswers, www.answers.com, 2010; The TalkOrigins Archive, www.talkorigins.org, 2006

77. Fiction.

78. Michael Benton, *Kingfisher Factfinder: Dinosaurs* (book), 2001

79. 'Fossil of Dog-Sized Horned Dinosaur Unearthed in China', National Geographic News, http://news.nationalgeographic.com, 2002; 'New Dinosaur Related to *Triceratops*', Science Daily, www.sciencedaily.com, 2002; California Academy of Sciences, www.calacademy.org, 2005

80. '*Tyrannosaurus rex* Was a Slowpoke', National Geographic News, http://news.nationalgeographic.com, 2002

81. A History of Dinosaur Hunting and Reconstruction, www.dinohunters.com, 2007; University of California Museum of Paleontology, www.ucmp.berkeley.edu, 2010

82. Fiction.

83. Fiction.

84. Fiction.

85. 'Revealed: Australia's Very Own Little Tyrannosaur', *The Sydney Morning Herald* (newspaper), Sydney, Australia, 26 March 2010

86. 'Snake Preyed on Baby Dinosaurs', *The Sydney Morning Herald* (newspaper), Sydney, Australia, 3 March 2010

87. 'Nothing Dull about an Orange Dinosaur', *The Sydney Morning Herald* (newspaper), Sydney, Australia, 28 January 2010

88. 'Dinosaurs "Lucky" Crurotarsan Predators Killed off by Volcanoes, Study Finds', News.com.au, www.news.com.au, 2010

89. Fiction.

90. Encyclopædia Britannica Online, www.britannica.com, 2010

91. Encyclopædia Britannica Online, www.britannica.com, 2010

92. Enchanted Learning, www.enchantedlearning.com, 2010

93. Enchanted Learning, www.enchantedlearning.com, 2010

94. Fiction.

95. Fiction.

96. 'Iguanodon', Beverly Eschberger, Suite101.com, www.suite101.com, 2000; Enchanted Learning, www.enchantedlearning.com, 2010

97. 'Runway Found for Flying Reptiles', BBC News, http://news.bbc.co.uk, 2009

98. *Encarta Encyclopedia* (CD), 1999

99. 'Titanosaurs – The Last of the Sauropods', Bob Strauss, About.com, http://dinosaurs.about.com, 2010; Queensland Museum, www.qm.qld.gov.au, 2010; 'Found! Australia's Largest Dinosaurs', ABC News in Science, www.abc.net.au, 2007

100. Fiction.

101. Steve Parker, *The Age of Dinosaurs: Dinosaurs and Birds,* (book), 2000; ABC Science, www.abc.net.au, 1998

102. Michael Benton, *Kingfisher Factfinder: Dinosaurs* (book), 2001; Dinosaurs for Kids, www.kidsdinos.com, 2010; Steve Parker, *The Age of Dinosaurs: Dinosaurs and Birds,* (book), 2000

Sources

103. Steve Parker, *The Age of Dinosaurs: Dinosaurs and Birds*, (book), 2000; Enchanted Learning, www.enchantedlearning.com, 2010; Michael Benton, *Kingfisher Factfinder: Dinosaurs* (book), 2001

104. Fiction.

105. Adam Hibbert, *Dangerous Dinosaurs* (book), 2006; The Dinosaur Interplanetary Gazette, www.dinosaur.org, 2006

106. Mick Manning and Brita Granström, *Dinomania: Things to Do with Dinosaurs* (book), 2001; 'The Poop on Dinos – Fossilized Dinosaur Dung – Includes Information on Coprolite', *Science World* (magazine), http://findarticles.com, United States of America, October 1998

107. *First Dinosaur Encyclopedia*, 1997; *The Penguin Historical Atlas of the Dinosaurs*, 1996

108. Fiction.

109. *First Dinosaur Encyclopedia*, 1997; Scott Hocknull and Dr Alex Cook, *Amazing Facts about Australian Dinosaurs* (book), 2006; Museum Victoria, http://museumvictoria.com.au, 2010

110. Adam Hibbert, *Dangerous Dinosaurs* (book), 2006; 'Pterodaustro', Bob Strauss, About.com, http://dinosaurs.about.com, 2010

111. 'Oldest Dinosaur Burrow Discovered', BBC Earth News, http://news.bbc.co.uk, 2009

112. 'Feathers Tied to Origin of Dinosaurs', MSNBC Digital Network: Science and Technology, www.msnbc.msn.com, 2009

113. 'First Horned Dinosaur from Mexico: Plant-Eater Had Largest Horns of Any Dinosaur', Science Daily, www.sciencedaily.com, 2010

114. Fiction.

115. 'Teenage *T. Rex*'s Monstrous Growth', BBC One-Minute World News, http://news.bbc.co.uk, 2004

116. 'Dinosaur "Lost World" Discovered', BBC News Online, http://news.bbc.co.uk, 1998; 'First Dinosaur Embryo Skin Discovered', Science A Go Go, www.scienceagogo.com, 1998

117. 'Dino Reputation "Is Exaggerated"', BBC News, http://news.bbc.co.uk, 2005; 'Velociraptor's "Killing" Claws Were for Climbing', New Scientist, www.newscientist.com, 2009

118. 'Dinosaur-Chewing Mammals Leave Behind Oldest Known Tooth Marks', Science Daily, www.sciencedaily.com, 2010

119. Fiction.

120. Enchanted Learning, www.enchantedlearning.com, 2010

121. John Long, *Insiders: Dinosaurs* (book), 2007; David Norman and Angela Milner, *Collins Eyewitness Guides: Dinosaurs* (book), 1991

122. David Norman and Angela Milner, *Collins Eyewitness Guides: Dinosaurs* (book), 1991; Planet Dinosaur, http://planetdinosaur.com, 2010

123. David Norman and Angela Milner, *Collins Eyewitness Guides: Dinosaurs* (book), 1991; Planet Dinosaur, http://planetdinosaur.com, 2010

124. 'A Dinosaur Dance Floor', EurekAlert, www.eurekalert.org, 2008; 'Dinosaur "Dance Floor" Found in Arizona', National Geographic News, http://news.nationalgeographic.com, 2008

125. Fiction.

126. David Norman and Angela Milner, *Collins Eyewitness Guides: Dinosaurs* (book), 1991

127. Fiction.

128. 'Dinosaur Diet', Scholastic: Teachers, http://content.scholastic.com, 2010

129. David Norman and Angela Milner, *Collins Eyewitness Guides: Dinosaurs* (book), 1991; Michael Benton, *Kingfisher Factfinder: Dinosaurs* (book), 2001

130. Scott Hocknull and Dr Alex Cook, *Amazing Facts about Australian Dinosaurs* (book), 2006; Australian Museum, http://australianmuseum.net.au, 2009

131. Michael Benton, *Kingfisher Factfinder: Dinosaurs* (book), 2001; David Norman and Angela Milner, *Collins Eyewitness Guides: Dinosaurs* (book), 1991; 'Dinosaurs Got Cancer', BioEd Online, www.bioedonline.org, 2003

132. David Norman and Angela Milner, *Collins Eyewitness Guides: Dinosaurs* (book), 1991

133. Fiction.

134. David Norman and Angela Milner, *Collins Eyewitness Guides: Dinosaurs* (book), 1991; Helen Fields: Science Writer, http://heyhelen.com, 2010

135. Dinosaur Den, www.dinosaurden.co.uk, 2003

136. David Norman and Angela Milner, *Collins Eyewitness Guides: Dinosaurs* (book), 1991; 'Are Chinese Dinosaurs Dragons or Fakes?, Associated Content, www.associatedcontent.com, 2008; 'Dragons, Dinosaurs, and "Fiery Serpents"', Apologetics Press, www.apologeticspress.org, 2003

137. Caroline Bingham, *First Dinosaur Encyclopedia*, 2007; National Park Service, US Department of the Interior, www.nps.gov, 2004

138. Caroline Bingham, *First Dinosaur Encyclopedia*, 2007; Michael Benton, *Kingfisher Factfinder: Dinosaurs* (book), 2001

139. 'Ichthyosaur Found in School Vegie Patch', ABC News, www.abc.net.au, 2010

140. Fiction.

141. Legend of Nessie Official Website, www.nessie.co.uk, 2010; The Plesiosaur Site, www.plesiosaur.com.php, 2009

142. Scott Hocknull and Dr Alex Cook, *Amazing Facts about Australian Dinosaurs* (book), 2006; Michael Benton, *Kingfisher Factfinder: Dinosaurs* (book), 2001

143. John Long, *Dinosaurs of Australia* (book) 1989; Caroline Bingham, *First Dinosaur Encyclopedia*, 2007; 'Giant Roach Fossil Found in Ohio Coal Mine', National Geographic News, http://news.nationalgeographic.com, 2001

144. Fiction.

145. Scott Hocknull and Dr Alex Cook, *Amazing Facts about Australian Dinosaurs* (book), 2006; Michael Benton, *The Penguin Historical Atlas of the Dinosaurs* (book), 1996; Dr David Norman, *The Illustrated Encyclopedia of Dinosaurs* (book), 1985; John Long, *Dinosaurs of Australia* (book) 1989

146. Michael Benton, *The Penguin Historical Atlas of the Dinosaurs* (book), 1996; Michael Benton, *Kingfisher Factfinder: Dinosaurs* (book), 2001; ABC News in Science, www.abc.net.au, 2003

147. Phil Bell and Eric Snively, 'Polar dinosaurs on parade: a review of dinosaur migration', *Alcheringa: An Australasian Journal of Palaeontology*, vol. 32 (3), 2008

148. Dinosaurs for Kids, www.kidsdinos.com, 2010; Melbourne Museum, http://museumvictoria.com.au, 2010

149. Fiction.

Sources

150. Fiction.

151. Caroline Bingham, *First Dinosaur Encyclopedia*, 2007; HowStuffWorks.com, http://animals.howstuffworks.com, 2010

152. Michael Benton, *The Penguin Historical Atlas of the Dinosaurs* (book), 1996; John Long, *Insiders: Dinosaurs* (book), 2007; Vertebrate Paleontology at Insubria University, http://dipbsf.uninsubria.it; Enchanted Learning, www.enchantedlearning.com, 2010

153. Dr David Norman, *The Illustrated Encyclopedia of Dinosaurs* (book), 1985; Michael Benton, *Kingfisher Factfinder: Dinosaurs* (book), 2001

154. 'Paleontologists Teach Medical Students about Fossil Tumors', Science Daily, www.sciencedaily.com, 2006

155. Michael Benton, *The Penguin Historical Atlas of the Dinosaurs* (book), 1996; University of California Museum of Paleontology, www.ucmp.berkeley.edu, 2005; Dinosaurs for Kids, www.kidsdinos.com, 2010

156. Fiction.

157. Melbourne Museum, http://museumvictoria.com.au, 2010; Enchanted Learning, www.enchantedlearning.com, 2010

158. Michael Benton, *The Penguin Historical Atlas of the Dinosaurs* (book), 1996; David Fastovsky and David Weishampel, *Dinosaurs: A Concise Natural History* (book), 2009

159. Fiction.

160. Luxury Watch Report, www.luxurywatchreport.com, 2009; MSNBC Digital Network, www.msnbc.msn.com, 2010

161. Michael Benton, *The Penguin Historical Atlas of the Dinosaurs* (book), 1996; Dr George Johnson's Backgrounders, http://txtwriter.com, 2008

162. *Encarta Encyclopedia* (CD), 1999; University of California Museum of Paleontology, www.ucmp.berkeley.edu, 2006; Women in Science, www.sdsc.edu, 1997

163. Dino Data, www.dinodata.org, 2010; 'Crichtonsaurus', Bob Strauss, About.com, http://dinosaurs.about.com, 2010

164. 'Attenborosaurus', Bob Strauss, About.com, http://dinosaurs.about.com.htm, 2010; The Plesiosaur Directory, http://plesiosaurnews.wordpress.com, 2010

165. Fiction.

166. 'Cryolophosaurus', Bob Strauss, About.com, http://dinosaurs.about.com, 2010; Enchanted Learning, www.enchantedlearning.com, 2010

167. Fiction.

168. 'The 10 Strangest Dinosaur Names: Dinosaur Names Even YOU Couldn't Come Up With!', Bob Strauss, About.com, 2010; 'Colepiocephale', Bob Strauss, About.com, http://dinosaurs.about.com, 2010; Thescelosaurus, www.thescelosaurus, 2010

169. Fossilsmith Studios, www.triunecommunications.com.html, 2005; The Children's Museum of Indianapolis, www.childrensmuseum.org, 2010; 'Bambiraptor', Bob Strauss, About.com, http://dinosaurs.about.com, 2010

170. 'Shuvuuia', Bob Strauss, About.com, http://dinosaurs.about.com, 2010; Luis V Rey's Art Gallery: Dinosaurs and Paleontology, www.luisrey.ndtilda.co.uk; American Museum of Natural History, www.amnh.org, 2010; Enchanted Learning, www.enchantedlearning.com, 2010

171. Fiction.

172. Walking with Dinosaurs (ABC, BBC), www.abc.net.au, 1999

173. Fiction.

174. Walking with Dinosaurs (ABC, BBC), www.abc.net.au, 1999

175. Fiction.

176. Australian Museum, http://australianmuseum.net.au, 2009

177. Fiction.

178. Fiction.

179. 'China Spends Billions to Study Dinosaur Fossils at Sites of Major Discoveries', *The Washington Post* (newspaper), Washington DC, USA, 26 January 2010

180. 'Chemical Remains of Dinobird Found', EurekAlert, www.eurekalert.org, 2010

181. 'Dinosaurs: How Long Did They Live?', Guardian News and Media, www.guardian.co.uk, 2009

182. Fiction.

183. Fiction.

184. Dinosaur National Monument – National Park Service, US Department of the Interior, www.nps.gov, 2000; 'New Dinosaur Rears Its Head in National Monument', National Park Service, US Department of the Interior, www.nps.gov, 2010

185. 'Epidendrosaurus', Bob Strauss, About.com, http://dinosaurs.about.com, 2010; 'Big Bad Bizarre Dinosaurs', National Geographic, http://ngm.nationalgeographic.com, 2007; National Geographic, http://animals.nationalgeographic.com.au, 2010

186. National Geographic, http://ngm.nationalgeographic.com, 2007; Enchanted Learning, www.enchantedlearning.com, 2010

187. Fiction.

188. My Jurassic Park, www.myjurassicpark.com, 2006

189. Michael Benton, *The Penguin Historical Atlas of the Dinosaurs* (book), 1996; Caroline Bingham, *First Dinosaur Encyclopedia*, 2007; Phil Bell and Eric Snively, 'Polar dinosaurs on parade: a review of dinosaur migration', *Alcheringa: An Australasian Journal of Palaeontology*, vol. 32 (3), 2008

190. 'Giant Dinosaur Footprints Found in Argentine "Jurassic Park" ', Yahoo News, http://news.yahoo.com, 2010

191. Scott Hocknull and Dr Alex Cook, *Amazing Facts about Australian Dinosaurs* (book), 2006

192. Fiction.

193. 'Eustreptospondylus', Bob Strauss, About.com, http://dinosaurs.about.com, 2010; Walking with Dinosaurs (ABC, BBC), www.abc.net.au, 1999

194. 'Jurassic Fast Food Was a Key to Giant Dinosaurs', Science Daily, www.sciencedaily.com, 2010

195. Fiction.

196. HowStuffWorks , http://animals.howstuffworks.com, 2010; Enchanted Learning, www.enchantedlearning.com, 2010; 'Torosaurus', Bob Strauss, About.com, http://dinosaurs.about.com, 2010

197. Palaeontological Society of the Peace, www.gprc.ab.ca, 2009

198. Fiction.

199. Fiction.

200. 'Dinosaur Mummy Found With Fossilized Skin and Soft Tissues', Science Daily, www.sciencedaily.com, 2007; 'Mummified Dinosaur Found by Tyler Lyson '06 Is Ready for Its Closeup', Swarthmore College News, www.swarthmore.edu, 2007; 'Mummified Dinosaur Slowly Being Revealed', Fox News, www.foxnews.com, 2008

201. Fiction.

Sources

202. Walking with Dinosaurs (ABC, BBC), www.abc.net.au, 1999; 'How Many Insect Species Are There?', The Science Show: ABC Radio National, www.abc.net.au, 27 April 2002; 'How Many Fish in the Sea? About 20,000 Species', CTV News, www.ctv.ca, 2010; Burt Monroe and Charles Sibley, *Distribution and Taxonomy of Birds of the World* (book), 1991

203. Enchanted Learning, www.enchantedlearning.com, 2010; 'New Dinosaur Was Nut-Cracking "Parrot"', National Geographic News, http://news.nationalgeographic.com, 2009

204. Enchanted Learning, www.enchantedlearning.com, 2010; 'Styracosaurus', Bob Strauss, About.com, http://dinosaurs.about.com, 2010

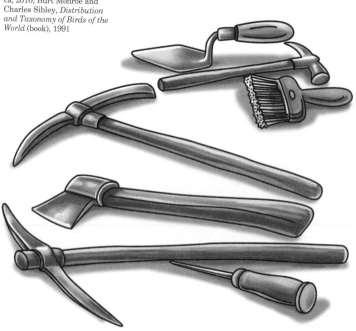

iNVENTiONS

1

One of the most frequently used objects in the home is the toilet. Throughout history, there have been various methods of disposing of human waste products, but thankfully, over time, more hygienic ways have become readily available. The very first flushable lavatory was invented in the mid-19th century by a man named Thomas Crapper!

 ✓ **FACT** **OR** **FICTION**

2 In today's society, it is hard to imagine a home without the constant presence of the television. Designs have altered drastically over the past couple of decades and the terms Plasma Screen, High Definition and Widescreen are commonplace. However, the first (and much less complex) television was not invented until the late 1920s by a Scottish engineer named John Logie Baird.

 FACT **OR** **FICTION**

Freaky Fact or Fiction

3

In 1957, Australian lecturer and rocket-fuels chemist Dr David Warren invented the first machine that was able to record flight data and sound from within the cockpit of a plane. This machine is virtually indestructible and has proven essential when trying to discover what happened when a flight has a disastrous ending. This machine's name is the ARL Flight-Memory Unit but is more commonly known by its nickname, The Black Box!

✓ FACT OR FICTION

4 Bullet-proof vests are in common use across the globe for law-enforcement officers. These magnificent garments are made of Kevlar, a product which is five times stronger than steel and remarkably light considering! Kevlar was invented by a man named Stephen Kevlar, who patented it in 1966. It is also used in the making of cables, brakes, parachutes and various sporting items including skis.

 ✓ **FACT**   **OR**   **FICTION**

Freaky Fact or Fiction

5 It seems that in our modern age, the mobile telephone or cell phone has become essential to each and every owner. Some people even insist that they couldn't live without theirs! However, it wasn't so long ago that you had to be in a specific location to answer a call.

The first telephone was invented by Alexander Graham Bell in 1876.

 ✓ **FACT**   **OR**   **FICTION**

6

Serendipity is a word that describes an instance where a pleasant discovery is made by accident. Such serendipity occurred in 1928 when Alexander Fleming noticed that some mould had killed off some bacteria in a petri dish. This led him to discover the fantastic effect penicillin could have, and the antibiotic drug has since had phenomenal success curing many basic illnesses.

✓ **FACT**   **OR**   **FICTION**

7

Most people love the indulgence of chocolate and some are even addicted to it! Chocolate has been around for hundreds of years and it comes from the cocoa bean. The English word 'chocolate' is derived from the ancient Aztec word 'xocoatl', which translates to 'warm and bitter liquid'! Is your mouth watering yet?

✓ **FACT**   **OR**   **FICTION**

8 Today, music can be found in many forms: on CD, on radio, downloadable from the internet and stored on portable music players. But the very first recording of sound was all down to Thomas Edison, who made a phonograph recording in 1877. The first words he recorded were 'Goodness me, I do hope this thing works!'

 ✓ **FACT** **OR** **FICTION**

9

The trombone is part of the brass family of musical instruments. The name comes from the Italian word for trumpet 'tromba' and the suffix '-one', meaning large. It was invented in 1450 but it was originally called a sackbut. 'Trombone' has a much nicer sound to it, don't you think?

✓ FACT OR FICTION

Inventions

10 Anyone who has a cat that generally lives indoors will know all about the convenience of a cat litter tray. For a long time, sand was the most often-used substance in these trays. In the 1940s, a man named Edward Lowe came up with the idea of using absorbent clay instead, so it was much easier to maintain. Easier than training a cat to flush the human toilet, at least!

 FACT **OR** **FICTION**

11

The first karaoke machine was invented by a Japanese man named Daisuke Inoue in the 1970s, although the social aspect of singing in public had been around for a long time before that. The word 'karaoke' comes from the Karaoke mountain ranges in Japan where an annual karaoke competition takes place every summer.

✓ **FACT**   OR   **FICTION**

12

The basic design for a zip fastener was originally in the form of a row of hooks, designed in 1893 by an engineer from Chicago, USA, named Whitcomb Judson. However, this was rather unreliable and a Swedish man named Gideon Sundback altered the design by using a series of cups that locked together. The name 'Zip' actually comes from a type of boot (the Zipper), which had this fastener on it.

✓ **FACT** **OR** **FICTION**

13

Wilhelm Röntgen was the very first man to win the Nobel Prize for Physics in 1901. He was the man who invented X-rays when he discovered that cathode rays could pass through just about anything. His discovery was made in 1895 and just 10 years later, X-ray specs were available in stores across Germany!

✓ **FACT** **OR** **FICTION**

14

Another winner of the Nobel Prize for Physics was Guglielmo Marconi, an Italian whose experiments led to the discovery of radio waves. Not only did this pave the way for radio broadcasts but it also started the wireless telegraph system, which helped ships communicate over the seas.

✓ **FACT** **OR** **FICTION**

Freaky Fact or Fiction

15 Today, it is rare to walk down the street or travel on public transport without seeing somebody listening to their iPod. This device for playing MP3 music files was designed and created by Steve Jobs and Apple Inc. in 2001. They are now currently working on a new version which will incorporate 'scratch and sniff'.

 ✓ **FACT** **OR** **FICTION**

16

Mobile phones, or cell phones, have come a long way since their birth. The first one was created by Bell labs in 1979 and had a rather large battery attached – not the sort of thing you could slip into your pocket! In 1991, the mobile phone became digital thanks to a system created by Groupe Spécial Mobile. These devices could change sound waves into a digital form for transmission by radio.

✓ **FACT** **OR** **FICTION**

Freaky Fact or Fiction

17

In 1998, satellites surrounding the earth were able to connect mobile or cell phone users across the planet – even in the most hard-to-reach places. This was especially helpful to those who didn't have mobile phone base stations nearby. The company Iridium Satellite LLC uses 66 satellites, each travelling around the world every 100 minutes!

 FACT   **OR**   **FICTION**

18

The compact disc (CD) was created when two companies worked together. Phillips and Sony produced a disc that could store music files and could be read using a laser. It took many years of hard work and lots of trial and error, but by 1982, the first commercially released CDs were available. These were Duran Duran's *Rio* and the soundtrack to the movie *Footloose*.

✓ **FACT** **OR** **FICTION**

Freaky Fact or Fiction

19

Counterfeit-proof money was developed by the CSIRO (Commonwealth Scientific and Industrial Research Organisation) in Australia. In 1988, the first plastic-laminated $10 banknote was released in Australia after 20 years of research. A special registration watermark makes the notes much more difficult to copy. The plastic nature of the money ensures a longer life span than ordinary paper notes.

 ✓ FACT   **OR**   **FICTION**

20

Although a notion only dreamt of by science-fiction writers for generations, 'Virtual Reality' became real in the 1980s. The 'Data Glove', which helps the wearer interact with an imaginary world, was originally created in 1982 by a US musician named Tom Zimmerman for the purpose of turning hand movements into musical data.

 FACT   **OR**   **FICTION**

Freaky Fact or Fiction

21 Hubert Cecil Booth was witness to a bizarre attempt to clear away dust and litter at St Pancras Station, London. The cleaners were *blowing* the mess away. Hubert realised it would be far more convenient to make a machine that sucked the dirt up and stored it, so he invented the vacuum cleaner in 1901. As the first designs were very bulky, he provided a door-to-door service with his contraption on his horse-drawn carriage.

✓ **FACT**   OR   **FICTION**

22

Just about everyone has had a teddy bear at one point in their life, but did you know that they were named after the US president Theodore 'Teddy' Roosevelt after he famously refused to kill an innocent baby bear during a hunting trip in 1902? A manufacturer designed a cuddly toy shaped like a bear and called it 'Teddy's Bear'.

✓ FACT OR FICTION

Freaky Fact or Fiction

23 When you are going on a long journey or you're having a picnic, it is often handy to have a thermos flask with you. The flask is able to keep its contents at a reasonably maintained temperature for a long period of time. It was invented by German Reinhold Burger in 1904 but only after being inspired by a similar but less useful product designed by British scientist, James Dewar.

 ✓ FACT OR FICTION

24

Although the first lie-detector was created by a European psychologist named Max Wertheimer in 1904, it wasn't until 1921 that a more precise version was made by an American named John Larson. Its official name is a polygraph and it measures the amount of sweat produced when someone is lying and can detect tell-tale signs like bodily twitches and stutters.

✓ **FACT**   **OR**   **FICTION**

25

Two brothers named Wilbur and Orville Wright became pioneers of controlled flying when they invented the very first plane – a vehicle that could carry a man through the air and be controlled by the pilot. This first flight occurred in December 1903 but only lasted for 12 seconds.

✓ FACT   OR   FICTION

26

When trying to apply logic to a problem, there are many ways to analyse the data. The Venn Diagram is one of those methods and it was invented by a British man called John Venn in 1881. The diagram consists of two or more circles which can overlap, showing how different things can share similar attributes. So, if one circle represented boys in a class of pupils, another represented children with curly hair and a third represented the ability to sing, the area where all three circles overlap would represent curly-haired boys who can sing.

✓ **FACT** **OR** **FICTION**

27

James Hargreaves was a spinner and weaver who lived near Lancashire in the UK. In the 1760s he invented a machine that could spin many threads at the same time, rather than one at a time, as had been the practice for a long time. The machine was called the spinning jenny. Thanks to its speed, it improved productivity in the textile industry.

 ✓ FACT OR FICTION

28

The spinning jenny was only the beginning! In 1769, Richard Arkwright advanced the machine to produce the water frame, which was powered by water and could produce much stronger thread. Arkwright's invention helped begin the factory-based system of production. Arkwright was knighted in 1786 for his efforts. He originally started out his career as a maker of wigs!

✓ **FACT** **OR** **FICTION**

29

The sparkling wine known as champagne is an alcoholic drink popular at times of celebration. Although the invention of this beverage is often attributed to a wine-loving French monk named Dom Pérignon, some people say sparkling wine had been produced in Britain for some time before this. There are many myths and legends surrounding the history of one of the most celebrated alcoholic drinks, but maybe that is all part of the charm!

✓ FACT   OR   FICTION

30 The binary system has been around in theory for thousands of years, dating back to early Chinese philosophy. Despite its early origins, the system was only adapted for mathematical use in 1679 by a philosopher from Germany named Gottfried Leibniz. It's a system using only the numbers one and zero and is used constantly today in the form of computer language.

✓ **FACT** **OR** **FICTION**

Freaky Fact or Fiction

The umbrella is a very common object that is used for protection from rain and sun. Various designs have been around since about 1637, but the steel-ribbed structure so familiar to us all was designed in 1874 by an Englishman named Samuel Fox. We can only assume he had grown tired of those wet English summers!

✓ FACT   OR   FICTION

32 The barometer is a tool that can gauge the air pressure in the atmosphere. It was invented by an Italian friend of Galileo's named Evangelista Torricelli in 1643. The physicist placed some yeast-based liquid into a tube and noted how it rose and fell, depending on the air pressure. The name 'barometer' was given to it by a Frenchman named Edmé Mariotte in 1676.

 FACT **OR** **FICTION**

Freaky Fact or Fiction

33 The dictionary is a very important reference book. In 1623 an Englishman named Henry Cockeram compiled a book that listed the meanings of a variety of words, but only those he considered to be obscure compared to those used in everyday language. In 1755 a new and improved dictionary, written by Samuel Johnson, was published. This was updated with modern terms such as 'plastic', 'snorkel' and 'bling'.

 ✓ FACT   OR   FICTION

34

George Stephenson was an engineer who was born in England in 1781. On 27 September 1825, Stephenson's own steam railway locomotive made its first journey between Darlington and Stockton, covering 24 km (15 mi). George was also the inventor of the dance known as 'The Loco-motion'.

 ✓ **FACT** **OR** **FICTION**

35 Although many scientists attempted to create a decent fire-producing implement for the home, it wasn't accomplished until 1827. In that year a British chemist called John Walker made a thin wooden stick tipped with chemicals which ignited when brushed against sandpaper. He named this stick a 'Friction Light' although now we simply call it a match.

 FACT **OR** **FICTION**

36

Braille is a very delicate system of writing. Letters, words and numbers are created on a surface through a series of raised dots. Blind people can read Braille by touching it. In 1829 it was invented by a Frenchman named Louis Braille, who had been blinded when he was a young boy in an accident at home. Louis was not going to let this ruin his life and he also became an accomplished pianist and cellist.

 FACT   **OR** **FICTION**

37

Not everyone has a goat, so it's not so simple for everyone to keep their lawns tidy. Unless, of course, you have a lawnmower! In 1830, the first lawnmower was invented by Edwin Budding and it was a crude machine with a cylindrical cutting device at the front and a large roller at the back. It was a rather heavy machine, but it got the job done.

✓ **FACT**   **OR**   **FICTION**

38

Morse code was invented by Samuel Morse from the USA in 1838. Mr Morse wanted to create a system of communication that was quick and easy to use and could be sent via electricity. So he made an alphabet equivalent using dots and dashes to represent each letter. It is fairly common knowledge that the distress signal SOS is represented as Dash Dash Dash, Dot Dot Dot, Dash Dash Dash.

✓ **FACT** **OR** **FICTION**

Freaky Fact or Fiction

39

You may be surprised at how useful polystyrene is. It isn't simply the material you might find securing delicate equipment in a box or a foam coffee cup; it is also used in the making of CD and DVD cases. The durable product we use today was invented by American chemist Robert Dreisbach in 1937, but he got the idea from a German called Eduard Simon whose invention in 1839 was similar but problematic due to its brittle nature.

✓ **FACT** **OR** **FICTION**

40

For more than 150 years, the physical delivery of mail (rather than the electronic kind) has been paid for through the use of postage stamps. The idea came from an Englishman named Rowland Hill in 1840. He wanted a system of mail delivery that could be accessed by absolutely anybody and so introduced the idea of a fixed price for posting. The very first stamp was called the Jenny Black.

✓ **FACT** **OR** **FICTION**

41 Linoleum is a hard-wearing floor covering used in many homes and businesses today. It is durable and easy to clean. It was invented by a British man called Frederick Walton who worked in the rubber industry. Linoleum is made from a variety of natural ingredients including linseed oil, cork powder and wood flour, which means it is surprisingly environmentally friendly.

 ✓ FACT OR FICTION

42

Most people in the world are very familiar with the keyboard on their computer. The layout dates back to the invention of the typewriter in 1868, when three men – Christopher Latham Sholes, Carlos Glidden and Samuel Soulé – wanted to create a machine that could help someone write efficiently without getting writer's cramp! The 'Qwerty' keyboard is laid out in such a way because the arms attached to each letter were less likely to jam.

 ✓ **FACT** **OR** **FICTION**

43

A rotary clothes line is great for drying washing in fine weather. The first one was designed and made by Lance Hills from Adelaide, Australia. He was a motor mechanic who was keen to stop using up so much space with one long washing line. He made his 'Hills Hoist' out of scrap metal before production was taken up.

✓ FACT   OR   FICTION

44

It has been estimated that there are more than 750 million motorised vehicles in the world. Back in 1885, this notion would have been mind-blowing! The first car was invented by a German called Karl Benz and it was a simple three-wheeled carriage powered by an internal combustion engine, although it looked more like a large tricycle than the cars we know today.

 ✓ **FACT** **OR** **FICTION**

45

Bondi Beach is the home of the invention of the life-saving reel. This is a long cord that attaches to the life-saver, who can enter the water and is then able to be reeled back in with the rescued person. The prototype model was made by Lyster Ormsby but the fully-working machine was built in 1906 by GH Olding. The first successful rescue using the reel was in January 1907, when a young Charlie Kingsford Smith was saved. (He went on to become a pioneering aviator.)

 ✓ FACT   OR   FICTION

46

Mixing gas and electricity can have surprising results. In 1910, a physicist from France named Georges Claude tried an experiment with neon gas and he discovered that it lit up when electricity was passed through it. Since then, neon signs have been lighting up streets in cities and towns across the globe.

✓ **FACT** **OR** **FICTION**

47

Scrabble is a board game that is loved by millions of people worldwide and is now playable online as well as in the original format. It was invented by Alfred Butts in 1931. He was an unemployed man at the time and, although initially rejected by various companies, he teamed up with James Brunot before selling the idea to Selchow & Righter. Before the game was named Scrabble, it was known as Criss-Cross and Lexico!

 ✓ FACT **OR** **FICTION**

48

Bubble gum has been around since the late 1920s and was invented by a man working for a chewing gum company. He was an accountant at the time but he wanted to make a gum that was more fun to chew, so he produced bubble gum. The magic ingredient was part of the rubber plant, which makes the gum stretchy.

 ✓ **FACT**   **OR**   **FICTION**

Freaky Fact or Fiction

49

Tea is one of the oldest and most loved beverages mankind has known. It is grown in a variety of countries around the world, including India and China, and there are many different blends and varieties. The tea bag, though, was only invented at the beginning of the 20th century when a New York salesman named Thomas Sullivan made individual bags to give to customers as samples. Instead of opening the bags, people just poured hot water on top!

 ✓ **FACT**   **OR**   **FICTION**

50

Thermal sterilisation of food sounds very complicated but basically it means that food in cans is safe to eat. At the end of the 18th century a Frenchman named Nicolas Appert came up with a way of storing food in sealed containers. The first canning factory opened in 1804 and tinned food was used by the British Navy in 1813. However, the first decent can-opener wasn't invented until 1858! Let's hope the food stayed fresh for that long!

✓ FACT OR FICTION

51 British inventor George Cayley began designing and building gliders in 1808. In 1853 he built the first triplane glider. It carried a passenger 275 m (900 ft). However, George was not willing to act as a guinea pig, so he got his coachman to take the flight instead. Thankfully, the flight was successful.

 ✓ **FACT** **OR** **FICTION**

52 **T**he hovercraft is a fascinating vehicle that can travel on land and water – truly the first man-made amphibious vehicle! It was invented in Britain in 1955 by Christopher Cockerell, but the first working model was only 762 mm (2 ft 6 in), used a model aircraft engine and was made of balsa wood. Not quite big enough for humans to travel in!

 ✓ FACT **OR** **FICTION**

Freaky Fact or Fiction

53

The most successful revolving pistol was invented in 1835 by an American named Samuel Colt. It was used by the Texas Rangers who wanted a sturdy and reliable weapon when the war between the Mexicans and the Americans broke out in 1846. Samuel also decided to make them in a variety of colours including blue, yellow, pink and a camouflage pattern.

 ✓ FACT

 OR

 FICTION

54

In 1943 Jacques-Yves Cousteau designed the aqualung for breathing under water. There were a few misfires during the process of invention, but he teamed up with Émile Gagnan who was an expert when it came to gas appliances. Gagnan suggested using nitrous oxide instead of oxygen, and the aqualung was born.

 FACT OR **FICTION**

Freaky Fact or Fiction

55

The first knitting machine was invented by William Lee in 1589. Mr Lee was a member of the clergy and the wooden apparatus was called the 'stocking frame'. William was so proud of his machine, but sadly, Queen Elizabeth I was not so impressed because she thought it would make a lot of hand-knitters unemployed!

✓ **FACT** **OR** **FICTION**

56

The pneumatic tyre was designed in 1887 by Scotsman John Boyd Dunlop when he wanted to make something for his son's tricycle to make it more comfortable for riding. A previous type of tyre had been invented by RW Thomson in 1846 but Dunlop used a more durable rubber and an inner tube. Dunlop's real job was as a trapeze artist in a circus before he found fame with his tyre.

 FACT **OR** **FICTION**

Freaky Fact or Fiction

57 **M**oving pictures were the desire of many keen-minded inventors. One man who tried his hardest was William Friese-Greene from Britain. In 1889 he claimed he could project images that gave the illusion of movement. The very first moving images were of four clowns having a custard pie–throwing contest in Trafalgar Square, London. However, this was not deemed a great success and in 1895 a far more successful motion picture was created by the Lumiere brothers.

✓ **FACT** **OR** **FICTION**

Inventions

58

Today, most people have some form of camera, even small ones inside their phones. Although basic forms of photographic equipment had been played with since 1814, the development of photographic film and celluloid was pioneered by George Eastman who founded the Kodak Company and brought out the Kodak camera in 1888. Despite his genius, George never finished school. He was a high school drop-out!

 FACT **OR** **FICTION**

Freaky Fact or Fiction

59

Holograms are incredibly cool 3D images created through the use of lasers. They were first designed by Hungarian engineer Dennis Gabor, who went on to win the 1971 Nobel Prize for physics. He worked as a professor at the Imperial College in London, which named one of their accommodation halls after him.

 FACT **OR** **FICTION**

60

Steamboats were the idea of a young man named Robert Fulton from the USA. Inspired by James Watt's steam engine, Fulton was still a teenager when he began applying Watt's ideas to a paddleboat. The first test failed when the boat sank, but it didn't stop him from pursuing his dream. He went on to design Napoleon Bonaparte's Nautilus submarine!

 ✓ **FACT** **OR** **FICTION**

61

The boomerang was made by Australian Aborigines as a hunting tool. The returning boomerang was also made for hunting as well as play and competitions. When flung through the air at a passing flock of birds, the returning boomerang would hit the birds and fly back due to the curvature of the wood. The startled birds could then be caught by a hunting party. The name comes from the Turuwul Tribe of the Georges River area. It literally means 'curved throwing stick'.

✓ **FACT**   **OR**   **FICTION**

62 Stainless steel can be found in just about every household. Stainless steel is one type of alloy steel. The first successful alloy steel was designed by Robert Abbott Hadfield from Sheffield in England, and he patented it in 1883. He added carbon and manganese to iron to make it resistant to corrosion, or wearing away. Other alloy steels have carbon and other elements added to iron. Stainless steel has carbon and chromium added to iron, and may also contain other elements such as nickel. These days, most cutlery is made from stainless steel and can withstand most bumps, liquids and scratches.

 FACT **OR** **FICTION**

Freaky Fact or Fiction

63

One of the best-recognised names associated with sewing machines is Isaac Singer. However, Singer's machine actually borrowed from the design of fellow American inventor Elias Howe, infringing on his patent, so Singer had to pay royalties for all machines sold in the USA. Although Howe was first with his design in 1846, Isaac Singer's company was more successful.

✓ **FACT** **OR** **FICTION**

64

Ejector seats in planes were invented for fighter aircraft. They were designed by James Martin, whose company began a radical series of ejector seat tests in 1945. Early designs were simply a coiled spring beneath the seat but later on explosive devices were created to launch the chair away from the plane.

 FACT **OR** **FICTION**

65

When hot air balloons were being tested for the first time in France in 1783, animals were used as passengers. The two brothers who invented the hot air balloon, Joseph-Michel and Jacques-Étienne Montgolfier, eventually braved the journey in the basket, suspended beneath the large balloon made of paper.

✓ FACT OR FICTION

66

The jet engine was a major accomplishment in the history of flight. The brilliant idea came from Frank Whittle in 1928, although it took many years to 'take off'. It was not until the Second World War that the British government understood how essential it was to have better flying machines, and the British Air Ministry felt encouraged to back Whittle and his designs. On 15 May 1941, the first jet plane had its maiden flight, with Whittle's jet engine fitted in a Gloster aircraft.

✓ **FACT** **OR** **FICTION**

Freaky Fact or Fiction

On 8 July 1838, Ferdinand Von Zeppelin was born in Germany. His name is now famous as it was lent to the airships that he invented. Zeppelins were vast airships comprising a small carriage underneath a sturdy framed balloon filled with gases lighter than air, notably helium or hydrogen. More than 100 zeppelins were used for military purposes during the First World War. However, the Hindenburg disaster of 1937, in which a balloon ignited and crashed to earth, stopped the production of zeppelins until it recommenced in the 1990s for sightseeing flights.

 FACT **OR** **FICTION**

68

In 1939, the Nobel Prize for Physics went to Ernest Orlando Lawrence. He was the man who invented the cyclotron. His prototype was very small and made of wax, brass and wire. A cyclotron is a machine that can harness the wind in order to power washing machines and spin-dryers.

 ✓ **FACT** **OR** **FICTION**

Freaky Fact or Fiction

69

The gas mask was invented in 1912 by Garrett Augustus Morgan, an African American from Ohio. Although the design has changed a lot between then and now, the initial safety hood was a big hit, especially when he demonstrated its use after a tunnel explosion in 1916 and he saved a number of lives. He also invented the traffic light system – more of that later!

✓ FACT   OR   FICTION

70

Nylon is a synthetic fibre made by Wallace Hume Carothers in the 1930s. It is man-made but produced from various materials from nature. He created nylon while researching polymers (like silk or rubber) and their strength and durability. Nylon has been used to make stockings and parachutes, and also the bristles on toothbrushes.

✓ **FACT** **OR** **FICTION**

Freaky Fact or Fiction

71

When watching sport on television today, we are often amazed at the camerawork and detail we get to see. We witness the car race from within the vehicle and we can watch a tennis match as though we are on the court. This is all due to the Race-Cam, a compact and sturdy camera designed in 1979 by Geoff Healy, who was a television engineer for Australia's Channel Seven TV network.

 ✓ **FACT** **OR** **FICTION**

72

Although toasting bread has been a culinary delight for hundreds and hundreds of years, the first electric toasting machine was invented in the UK in 1893 by Crompton and Co. The first pop-up toaster was built in 1919 by Charles Strite who became frustrated with the frequency of burned toast.

 ✓ **FACT** **OR** **FICTION**

Freaky Fact or Fiction

73

Cluedo is a popular board game in which players try to decipher who is the murderer, which weapon was used and which room was the scene of the crime. This fascinating game of logic was invented by Anthony Pratt from Birmingham, England. The name Cluedo is based on the word 'clue' and the Latin word 'ludo', which means 'I play'. In some countries, the game is simply known as Clue.

 ✓ FACT   OR   FICTION

74

Roget's *Thesaurus* was a product of Dr Peter Roget's retirement. He found himself with time on his hands but he wanted to keep on working. Roget had been interested in linguistics for most of his life, so in retirement he spent a long time classifying English words and phrases. The book he produced could aid those learning English or those who wanted to get more out of the language and broaden their verbal skills. The whole job took him four years but the finished book has been around for more than 150 years!

 FACT **OR** **FICTION**

Freaky Fact or Fiction

75

If a plane makes an unscheduled landing, the passengers and crew need a way to get to safety. In 1965 Jack Grant was working as an Operations Safety Superintendent for Qantas airlines. He invented an escape slide which inflated in a matter of seconds and could also be used as a life raft if the emergency landing is in the sea. The slide rafts are now standard in all major aircraft, and even in some trains and buses.

✓ FACT OR FICTION

76 In 1919, George Hansburg from the USA invented the pogo stick – a simply designed toy that allows the 'rider' to bounce up and down while holding onto the handles. Although there are many stories surrounding the history, it is fairly common knowledge that the name is an acronym for Pounce On, Go Orbital.

 ✓ **FACT** **OR** **FICTION**

77

The escalator was not originally in the form we know it today. It was simply a sloping travelator designed by Jesse Reno. The moving stairway aspect was invented by George Wheeler and developed by Charles Seeberger who worked for the Otis Elevator Company. It was first exhibited in Paris in 1950.

✓ **FACT** **OR** **FICTION**

78

Australian winemaker Thomas Angove came up with the wine cask as an alternative to bottled wine. The prototype was made by South Australian company Angoves in 1965 and consisted of a laminated plastic bag housing the wine with a vacuum inside so the wine stayed at its peak flavour. Later versions included a tap nozzle (added by the Penfolds Company), which was later perfected by The Wynns Company in 1969.

✓ **FACT** **OR** **FICTION**

Freaky Fact or Fiction

79 Two great minds collided when the Post-It note was invented. Spencer Silver created a new form of adhesive and Art Fry applied it to a bookmark! Initially, the clever little sticky notes were distributed throughout the company (3M) but three years later, in 1980, they were available throughout the USA and, eventually, the world!

 ✓ FACT   OR   FICTION

80

The bionic ear is an amazing invention! It helps those with little or no hearing to hear once again. It was developed by a team at Melbourne University, Australia, headed by Professor Graeme Clark. Part of the device is implanted in the skull and the other is worn over the ear to analyse and process the sounds. This technology is now exported around the globe to help hundreds of thousands of people.

 FACT OR FICTION

Freaky Fact or Fiction

81

Vulcanised rubber is a form of tree sap which has been weatherproofed. This needed to happen because natural rubber tended to melt in heat or turn brittle in the cold. It was Charles Goodyear from Connecticut, USA, who made it resistant to extreme temperatures by putting it through a process of steaming over a period of time and adding sulfur.

 ✓ FACT **OR** **FICTION**

Inventions

82 In 1904, in Melbourne, Australia, William Ramsay created a boot polish, which had rather terrific properties. It was able to polish leather, preserve it and also restore any faded colour. William developed the polish while working in a small factory with his business partner Hamilton McKellan. In 1906, it was branded Kiwi Boot Polish and today is sold worldwide. It gets its name from the main ingredient, kiwi fruit.

 ✓ FACT   OR   FICTION

Freaky Fact or Fiction

83 The light bulb was developed by two bright sparks. One was Thomas Edison from the USA and the other was Joseph Swan from the UK. It was a combination of necessity, advances in science and coincidence that both men came up with the same idea. However, it was Swan who first thought of using a carbon filament within the bulb in 1878, a year before Edison.

 FACT OR **FICTION**

84

The first feature-length film was made in Australia in 1906, and was screened in Melbourne. Most films at the time were surprisingly short, averaging about 10 minutes. However, *The Story of the Kelly Gang*, written and directed by Charles Tait, went for well over an hour.

✓ **FACT** **OR** **FICTION**

Freaky Fact or Fiction

85

Granny Smith apples are perhaps the most famous and popular apples in the world. They are edible raw but also delicious when cooked in pies or crumbles. This specific blend of apple was discovered by Maria Ann Smith in Sydney, Australia; in 1868 when she grew a new type of apple from the leftovers of some Tasmanian French crab-apples. Since then, they have become known and loved as Granny Smith's.

 FACT **OR** **FICTION**

86

The very first rubber gloves were invented by an American surgeon named William Stewart Halsted in 1890. They were manufactured by the Goodyear Rubber Company. Gloves for household use were developed in 1925 by the Australian company, Ansell Rubber, and were made of latex. In 1964, the company developed a disposable rubber glove (much more hygienic!) specifically for use in surgery.

 ✓ FACT OR FICTION

87

Microsurgery began in the 1960s. Many scientists and surgeons were involved in pioneering a way of performing surgery on a microscopic level. Harry Buncke started his work in his own garage, as well as a laboratory at Stanford University, USA, and in 1964 reported that he was the first person to successfully replant a rabbit ear! Microsurgery has gone on to help incredible feats such as reattaching limbs and delicate eye-surgery. Various instruments were also created by Dr David Vickers from Brisbane, Australia, who made tiny little robots that worked inside the human body.

 ✓ FACT　　 **OR**　　 **FICTION**

88

Prior to the invention of the landmine detector, soldiers would simply be told to thrust the ground ahead of them with the tips of their bayonets. As you would expect, this caused a lot of damage when they eventually found one. So, during the Second World War, a soldier named Miller (whose full name was never recorded) created a device using a tuning coil and a wireless valve. These combined made an oscillator that could detect landmines beneath the earth. This was a very early form of landmine detector which was later replaced by a more accurate design by a Polish soldier, Lieutenant Józef Stanislaw Kozacki.

 ✓ FACT OR FICTION

89

The first cardiac pacemaker was designed as early as 1926 and was used to revive a newborn infant. The first attempted implant of a pacemaker was in October 1958 and the operation was performed by Swedish surgeon Ake Senning. The first successfully implanted pacemaker was devised by Wilson Greatbatch from New York, USA. The amazing device, when implanted inside the body, can regulate the heartbeat. The first implant was in October 1958 and the operation was performed by Swedish surgeon, Ake Senning.

✓ FACT OR FICTION

90

CR39 is a special kind of plastic which was originally used in the windshields of aircraft. However, in 1960 it was adapted for spectacles by Noel Roscrow of SOLA (Southern Operations of Light Aircraft), making the lenses more scratch-proof than regular glass.

✓ **FACT** OR **FICTION**

91

The Wiltshire StaySharp knife is a perfect tool for chefs and anyone who likes to spend a lot of time in their kitchen. It's a strong, useful knife that actually sharpens each time it is placed and withdrawn from its sheath due to an abrasive interior. It was created by an offshoot of Sir Frederick Wiltshire's company named 'The Wiltshire Cutlery Company'.

✓ **FACT**   **OR**   **FICTION**

92

Earle Dickson was inspired to invent the bandaid by his wife who frequently cut herself in the kitchen and complained that bandages would not stay on her busy hands. As an employee of Johnson & Johnson, he used his knowledge to create a bandage made up of adhesive tape, gauze and crinoline, which would stick over the flesh. It kept the wound protected without hindering the wearer from continuing their work. They have been around since 1721!

 FACT **OR** **FICTION**

93

Sheep shearing is a delicate and precise job and is seen as a great craft, but also as a sport in some places. It demands a firm grip, a keen eye and a steady hand, and was originally done with sharp shears. However, in 1877, Robert Savage and Frederick York Wolseley invented a mechanical shearer. In competition, it was a little slower than the speedy professionals with their blade shears, but it actually gave a much finer cut and took off more wool.

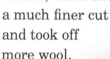

 ✓ **FACT**   **OR**   **FICTION**

94

The first solar-powered car was built by Englishman Alan Freeman in 1979. The first World Solar Challenge was held in 1987 in Australia. Solar-powered cars raced between Darwin (Northern Territory) and Adelaide (South Australia). The first winner took five days and eight hours to make the 3000-km (1864-mi) journey.

✓ **FACT** **OR** **FICTION**

95

Willis Carrier was an engineer from New York, USA, who came up with the idea of making a refrigeration unit which would actually cool down the air indoors. This involved designing a device that could extract the hot air from a room and pump cold air back in. The first air-conditioner was created in 1902 but has developed a huge amount over the past century and is now common in many buildings.

✓ FACT OR FICTION

96 **M**eccano is a wonderfully inventive building toy which comprises many strips of metal and plenty of nuts and bolts. These metal pieces could be constructed to make an infinite amount of new toys. It was devised by Frank Hornby of Liverpool, England, and has been a successful toy since 1901. Its original name was 'Mechanics Made Easy'.

✓ **FACT** **OR** **FICTION**

97

The safety razor came about because Mr Gillette of Brookline, Massachusetts, was **a)** concerned about safety and **b)** a salesman with a great idea. He created the disposable razor. It eliminated the need to sharpen a blade repeatedly for a good shave and enticed the users to buy new blades when they became blunt. His first disposable razors were made out of gold, so were very expensive.

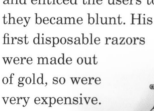

 FACT　　　**OR**　　　**FICTION**

98 Formica is a man-made material used in some floors and work surfaces. It was developed by Daniel O'Conor from Pittsburgh, Pennsylvania, in 1913. It gets its name from 'for mica', as mica was a very expensive mineral and something cheaper was needed. Although popular in the functional use of furniture, it was originally thought of for uses in vehicles.

✓ **FACT** **OR** **FICTION**

Freaky Fact or Fiction

Prior to the self-service supermarket, customers would go into a store and ask the attendant behind the counter for all their grocery needs. This would be time-consuming and a lot of hard work for that employee.

So, in 1916, Clarence Saunders from Memphis, Tennessee, opened a self-service store and then patented the idea for the supermarket, which we have come to know so well. His own chain was called 'Shoparama' and it is still in business today.

✓ **FACT**   **OR**   **FICTION**

100

The armoured tank is a large vehicle which is able to travel across different surfaces and pass over trenches by using its endless tracks, known as caterpillar tracks. This formidable machine is also armed with weapons. Although its invention was sometime around the First World War, various designs were being tried out in England and in Austria. However, the model close to the one we are familiar with today was created by William Tritton in 1915 and was nicknamed 'Little Willie'.

✓ **FACT** **OR** **FICTION**

101

Autopilot in planes is an amazing tool which maintains the flight level and the correct direction. Although it is merely an aid for the pilot, it is an essential one. In the early part of the 20th century, there were a number of varying inventions with the same ultimate purpose but the one that was patented was made by Frederick Meredith, from England, for the Royal Aircraft Establishment.

✓ **FACT** **OR** **FICTION**

102 **R**apid freezing was a creation of Clarence Birdseye, whose name we are familiar with to this day. In the 1920s, he designed a refrigeration machine which could flash-freeze food by using high pressure. He got the idea from watching Inuit people in Canada placing their freshly caught fish into ice to preserve them for longer.

 ✓ **FACT** **OR** **FICTION**

Freaky Fact or Fiction

103

Garrett Morgan, the African-American inventor of the gas mask, also invented the traffic lights system. Beforehand, crossroads would occasionally be manned by a policeman with a 'stop/go' sign, but Garrett witnessed a nasty accident in which a young girl was injured and he was inspired to come up with a new traffic management system – a T-shaped pole with three signals to make roads safer for motorists and pedestrians. The very first lights were used in Cleveland, Ohio.

✓ **FACT**   **OR**   **FICTION**

104

The Anglepoise lamp was invented in the early 1930s by George Carwardine from Bath in England. He came up with the idea while pondering the use of springs and how he could design a movable arm which could be flexible but rigid at the same time. The only thing is, he didn't consider the use of a lamp on one end until years after he had perfected the arm. Since then, it has been used in homes, offices and hospitals among other places.

✓ **FACT** **OR** **FICTION**

Freaky Fact or Fiction

105

Cat's eyes are the reflecting lights often seen in roads in places where there is low light at night. As the name suggests, the man who invented them, Percy Shaw from Yorkshire in England, was inspired when he saw a cat's eyes light up one foggy night. He later went on to become Prime Minister of England!

 FACT OR **FICTION**

106

Monopoly is one of the most popular board games in the world and there have been many different variations since the birth of the original version back in 1935. It was created by a man named Charles Darrow from Philadelphia, Pennsylvania, USA. His original prototype was painted onto an old tablecloth and he made all the little houses and hotels out of wood. He was the first board game creator to become a millionaire!

 FACT **OR** **FICTION**

Freaky Fact or Fiction

107

Parking meters serve a couple of purposes. Firstly, they make sure that parking in a busy town or city is easier for shoppers who normally couldn't park due to those who hogged a spot all day while at work. Secondly, they help raise money for the local council. The notion of a parking meter was thought up by Carl Magee in Oklahoma and a patent was applied for in 1935. He invented it because he was a traffic warden who was tired of having to memorise where all the cars had been during the day.

✓ **FACT**   **OR**   **FICTION**

108

Photocopiers are familiar objects in most offices around the world. Although they are the cause of much grief when they have their temperamental moments, they are incredibly efficient at saving time. Prior to the invention of the photocopier (by Chester Carlson from New York City in 1938), making copies of documents was much slower and was often done by hand!

✓ **FACT** **OR** **FICTION**

Freaky Fact or Fiction

109

The purpose of radar was not always the one we are familiar with today. Scottish inventor Robert Watson-Watt, a superintendent working for the British Scientific Survey of Air Defence, was originally asked to discover a way that radio waves could be used as a weapon against aircraft. He told his superiors that with the scientific knowledge of the time, this would be impossible. However, he did figure that radio waves could at least detect aircraft and so the radar was born.

✓ **FACT**   **OR**   **FICTION**

110 For cooks and chefs everywhere, teflon created a revolution and its non-stick substance redefined cooking techniques in kitchens across the globe. Roy Plunkett from Delaware, USA, worked for NASA in 1938 and was asked to find a substance suitable for cooking meats in space. Eventually, teflon was being used in a variety of kitchen utensils including the muffin pan and the frying pan.

✓ **FACT** OR **FICTION**

Freaky Fact or Fiction

111

Barcodes are featured on just about everything we buy these days. They were invented by two students in Pennsylvania named Bernard Silver and Norman Woodland. The two men worked on an idea of having a label on a supermarket product which could detail the information at the checkout. The barcode itself is a distant relation of morse code, with different combinations forming different sets of information. However, this also meant they had to invent a decent scanner too! The very first product scanned in the commercial area was a packet of chewing gum.

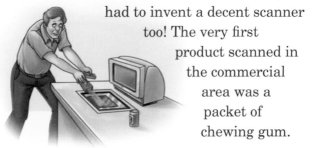

✓ **FACT**   **OR**   **FICTION**

Inventions

112

The ballpoint pen was invented by journalist Laszlo Biro and he patented his idea in 1943. Originally from Hungary, he moved to Argentina with his brother. Having noticed how fountain pens often leaked and blotted and how the ink used in printing presses seemed to be thicker, he decided to combine the two ideas to create a pen with ink that could be controlled through a roller ball at the tip. Interestingly, Laszlo had also worked as a sculptor and a hypnotist!

✓ FACT OR FICTION

Freaky Fact or Fiction

113

The instant camera was thought up by Edwin Land, who founded the Polaroid company in 1937. The company specialised in making filters to polarise light and reduce glare. These filters were very effective in sunglasses. However, when his daughter asked him why she had to wait so long for a photograph to be developed, he put his mind to making an instant camera. He patented the idea in 1948. Nowadays, the Polaroid camera has been surpassed by the digital camera, but for a long time, it was state-of-the-art technology.

✓ FACT OR FICTION

114

The microwave oven was another case of an inventor stumbling upon a new discovery. Percy Spencer was working with the British invention the magnetron, and finding ways to improve it. While working on it, he discovered that chocolate would melt in his pocket. Further tests proved that the microwaves coming from the magnetron were able to cook things remarkably quickly. He designed a machine that used these microwaves and called it the 'Radarange' – obviously, this name did not stick.

 FACT **OR** **FICTION**

Freaky Fact or Fiction

115

The slinky toy is such a simple design but has entertained people for generations. The inventor, Richard James from Pennsylvania, worked as an engineer in the US Navy. He came up with this idea for a toy when he noticed a torsion spring fall during a rough bout of weather at sea. After discussion with his wife, he eventually worked out what would be the best material to use to make a toy spring and what the right tension and length the coil should be. His wife named it 'Slinky' after their pet snake.

 FACT **OR** **FICTION**

116 Tupperware is a very successful range of plastic kitchenware and containers which has been around since the late 1940s. Durable, airtight and resistant to various forces, it has been the centrepiece of picnics, food storage and even shopping parties for a long time. It was designed by a man named Earl Tupper from Massachusetts, USA, and some of the designs have even turned up in the Museum of Modern Art in New York!

 FACT **OR** **FICTION**

Freaky Fact or Fiction

117 Lego is a worldwide phenomenon that has spawned many imitators. Godtfred Christiansen from Denmark was the son of a man who began a business making and selling wooden toys and other household objects. Christiansen was inspired to create a toy system of building blocks and he patented the design for the first Lego brick. Thanks to the advent of plastics and moulding machines, these bricks would become easy to produce on a mass level. The term 'Lego' comes from the Danish phrase *Leg Godt*, which means 'Play Well'.

 ✓ FACT **OR** **FICTION**

118 Microchips are in so many gadgets and machines today that we tend to forget they exist, but without them, we'd be living in a very different world! Jack Kilby from Dallas, Texas, in the US, was already working as an engineer when he was asked to figure out a way to make electronic components much smaller. The first microchip from Kilby's intricate designs was manufactured in 1961. He went on to work on harnessing solar energy.

✓ **FACT** **OR** **FICTION**

119

Original car seatbelts simply went over the lap and around the waist. This was not completely effective as the upper body was not restrained during a sudden impact. Nils Bohlin was working for the Volvo Company in Sweden in 1958 when he came up with the design which is now standard in all vehicles. This 'three-point' design stretches across the waist and also the shoulder to a secure clip by the hip.

 ✓ FACT OR FICTION

120 The lava lamp is one of those iconic products from the 1960s and '70s. It's a light that incorporates a mixture of wax and oil. The heat from the bulb melts the wax and causes it to rise within the casing; when it begins to cool, it solidifies and sinks again. The patterns created are almost hypnotic and a variety of colours and designs were produced. The lamp was developed by Crestworth Ltd in Dorset, England, although the owner, Craven Walker, was inspired by a prototype made of junk in a pub in Hampshire 15 years earlier!

✓ **FACT** **OR** **FICTION**

121

The waterbed was designed by Charles Hall from California in 1969. It is basically a mattress made of vinyl and filled with water (which could also be heated from beneath). Presumably, it was designed to provide a decent night's sleep. Earlier designs in the later half of the 19th century were unsuccessful because a material strong enough to hold the water had yet to be discovered. Some found that water moved a little too much and created too many 'waves', so the latest designs use a form of custard instead.

✓ FACT   OR   FICTION

122 iPods may be the rage now, but for many people in the 1980s, the personal stereo was the most entertaining accessory anyone could want. The first design came from Italy and was invented by Andreas Pavel in 1977. However, it wasn't this initial design that took off. The Walkman was designed a couple of years later by Sony and the greatest advantage was its ability to run on very little battery power. The head of Sony, Akio Morita, did not come up with the name though. He wanted a name like the 'Sound About', but it was his staff who came up with 'Walkman'.

 ✓ FACT **OR** **FICTION**

123

Spray-on skin was invented by Australian-based Dr Fiona Wood as an aid to help heal burnt skin. Skin cell regeneration was developed in the USA, but it was Dr Wood who pioneered a much speedier process which was used to great effect on victims of the Bali bombings in 2002. Dr Wood was awarded the Australian of the Year award in 2005.

 ✓ **FACT** **OR** **FICTION**

124 Football boot studs are one of those essential inventions that tend to be overlooked. For football players, they need their footwear to be able to give them support and a good grip in the turf. The big question is: who invented them? Well, that's open for debate because both Puma and Adidas claim the invention was their own. What makes the matter even more interesting is that the founders of each company are brothers – Rudolf and Adolf Dassler.

 ✓ FACT **OR** **FICTION**

Freaky Fact or Fiction

125

The 1980s are often remembered for the simple yet infuriating puzzle called the Rubik's Cube. This diabolically frustrating yet addictive game was devised by an interior designer from Hungary. It is basically a cube made up of smaller cubes, with each side representing a different colour. The cubes can be rotated around the axis in a variety of ways and can become confused awfully easily. The name comes from the acronym for the Hungarian words 'Rejtvény Ugyanakkor Bûvészet Idegroham Kocka', which translate to 'Puzzle Now Magic Brainstorm Cube'.

✓ **FACT** OR **FICTION**

126

The cotton gin is a machine that extracts the seeds from the cotton plant in order to get the fibre in a usable form. Basically, the machine uses a rotating cylinder to pass the cotton through a comb which catches all the seeds. It was invented in 1793 by an American engineer named Eli Whitney. His invention brought him great wealth and he was able to retire on the money he made at the age of 35.

✓ **FACT**   **OR**   **FICTION**

Freaky Fact or Fiction

127 During the Second World War, the people of Britain were issued with their very own bunkers which they could build in their gardens and hide in during an air raid. These shelters were delivered in a pack and the families would erect them in a dug-out pit away from the home. They were made out of corrugated steel and they were named after the inventor, Andrew Anderson.

✓ FACT OR FICTION

128

hen heading under the ocean, you don't always have to be equipped with a diving suit and oxygen tanks. Thanks to British scientist Edmond Halley (1656–1742), you can go beneath the water in a diving bell. Mr Halley made sure the submersible chamber could keep someone under water for at least an hour and a half. By sending weighted barrels of air down to the bell, a person could maintain a breathable atmosphere. Inventor Edmond Halley was also the astronomer who discovered Halley's Comet.

 ✓ **FACT** **OR** **FICTION**

Freaky Fact or Fiction

129

Since the days of early man, humans have sought to make music from various inventions. The piano is a musical instrument that has been changed and revolutionised over the years. Its history is long and varied, though the instrument that most closely resembles the modern piano was created around 1709 by Bartolomeo Cristofori. This machine was a harpsichord that played the notes softer or louder, depending on the pressure applied to the keys.

✓ **FACT** **OR** **FICTION**

130 Condensed milk was an idea thought up by American inventor Gail Borden midway through the 19th century. Borden was aware that children could become ill from drinking infected milk. Through a process that sterilised the milk by boiling it under a vacuum, he was able to make it safe to consume. The reason it is called condensed milk is because of the reduced water percentage, which makes it thicker. Borden assumed that this was what made the milk safer, but it was actually safer because the sugar stopped bacteria from forming in the milk.

 FACT **OR** **FICTION**

131

The elevator is a common device in most tall buildings and eliminates the use of stairs. It was first invented by American Elisha Otis in 1852. Although various forms had been designed previously, Otis' safety elevator promised to prevent accidents from happening. Sales were phenomenally high within the first year and soon Otis had a successful business.

✓ FACT OR FICTION

132

We have used clocks to monitor the time for centuries, but the first watch was a little larger than the ones we are familiar with today. It was a device roughly the size of a hamburger and had complicated clockwork mechanisms within. It was invented in the very early 16th century by Peter Henlein, who was a locksmith in Germany. Unlike later designs, his portable watch had no minute hand!

 ✓ **FACT** **OR** **FICTION**

133

Rabies is a nasty infection which can cause inflammation in the brain and can be found in various animals. It is often transmitted through an animal bite and needs to be treated quickly. Luckily, a vaccine was invented by French microbiologist Louis Pasteur in 1885. He proved his vaccine worked when saving a young boy's life after he had been bitten by a rabid dog.

 ✓ FACT   OR   FICTION

134

Insulin is something that the body produces. If your own body cannot create enough of it, you can become diabetic. Thankfully, in 1921, Charles Best and Frederick Banting from Canada discovered you could make insulin from the sap of the silver birch tree. Ever since, this plant-born insulin has helped sufferers of diabetes get through their lives relatively stress-free.

✓ **FACT** **OR** **FICTION**

135

The theremin is an electronic musical instrument invented in 1919 by a Russian named Leon Theremin. The machine has two antennas and produces a variety of weird and spooky noises similar to a wail or a dog's howl. It was often used to supply a creepy soundtrack to science-fiction films in the early 20th century. The weirdest thing about this instrument is that to play it, you don't actually have to touch it. You just wave your hands between the antennas!

✓ FACT OR FICTION

136

Many homes have some sort of video game console for people to play on, both adults and children. However, the very first video game was a little larger than what we are used to. The first game was designed by American physicist Willy Higinbotham in 1958 and it was a very simple tennis game in which the player had to control a 'ball' going back and forth over a 'net'. This invention made Willy a millionaire.

 FACT **OR** **FICTION**

Freaky Fact or Fiction

137

Genetic fingerprinting is a term used to describe how an individual can be identified simply from the DNA they leave behind them, in things such as hair fibres, blood or dead skin. Just like our fingerprints, everybody's DNA is completely different. This notion, which advanced police forensic procedures a huge step, was discovered by

an Englishman named Alec Jeffreys. The first crime solved using genetic fingerprinting was for a burglary in January 1999.

 ✓ **FACT** **OR** **FICTION**

138

In many cars you may have seen a device that locks into the steering wheel. This is an Anti-Theft Device, invented by Mosheh Tamir from Israel in 1985. Although there are many different deterrents to stop thieves from stealing cars such as alarms and electronic locks, the 'wheel-clamp' device is a very solid and visible one.

✓ **FACT** **OR** **FICTION**

Freaky Fact or Fiction

139 The snowboard is a relatively new invention. Despite the fact that a variety of basic snowboards had been invented and trialled throughout the 1960s, it was Robert Weber of Maryland, USA, who first patented a design. The snowboard is actually more closely linked to the surfboard and skateboard than skis as it applies the same techniques to control it.

✓ **FACT** **OR** **FICTION**

140

MRI stands for Magnetic Resonance Imaging. It is a machine that can search human body cells and discover any tissue that may be cancerous. It was invented by Raymond Damadian from New York in the early 1970s and has been a boon to the medical industry, preventing an incalculable number of early deaths. Over the years, the system has been improved and is now invaluable for many doctors and patients.

✓ **FACT** **OR** **FICTION**

Freaky Fact or Fiction

141

The pressure inside a bottle of fizzy drink is quite large – just shake one up and open it to see the proof (but not indoors or there will be quite a mess to clean up!). The plastic of a bottle has to be a certain strength in order to contain the pressure. A man named Nathaniel Wyeth determined that a plastic could be strengthened during its manufacture by stretching the fibres as it was being moulded. So, since Wyeth's discovery in 1973, we have had stronger plastic bottles to contain the fizz!

 ✓ **FACT** **OR** **FICTION**

142

You may have seen films in which the characters have to go through an old mine and have a wild ride in one of the railroad carts as it speeds through the tunnels. Well, although this looks like a huge amount of fun, it was also immensely practical. These railways were first used in the mines in the middle of the 16th century, making the work much easier. Before this rail system, miners had helium-filled balloons to carry the minerals to the surface.

✓ **FACT** **OR** **FICTION**

143 Many workmen have spirit levels in their toolkits. It's a very important device as it is able, through a simple method of aligning a bubble in a fixed tube of liquid, to determine whether an object is positioned perfectly level. Due to the nature of gravity, an air bubble will always find the highest place in a liquid. Although it is unsure exactly who invented the spirit level, it is believed to have first been used in 1661.

 FACT **OR** **FICTION**

144

Just about everybody has one or more socks. Lovely woolly knitted socks are just perfect for keeping your toes warm in the colder winter months. However, you may be surprised to discover that the knitted sock is much older than you may have realised. It has been discovered that Egyptians were often buried in their tombs while sporting their homemade socks. This is as far back as 450 BC!

✓ FACT OR FICTION

Freaky Fact or Fiction

145 You will probably have heard of the expression 'The Best Thing Since Sliced Bread'. Well, it does make you wonder what people said *before* Otto Rohwedder of Iowa, USA, invented the bread-slicing machine! He patented his idea in 1928, even though he'd been working on the machine since 1912. His machine not only sliced the bread but also wrapped it in plastic.

✓ **FACT**   OR   **FICTION**

146 Road surfaces come in a variety of forms but they are similar. There is asphalt, bitumen and tarmac. All are used in similar ways. Tarmac was invented in 1902 by Edgar Hooley from Nottingham, England. His invention originated from curiosity when he noticed that a road in the county of Derbyshire was unlike the other dusty tracks. When he asked why, he found a barrel of tar had spilled and solidified. It had been mixed with dirt to help it dry.

 ✓ **FACT** **OR** **FICTION**

147

Although the notion of an invisibility cloak seems to be only for the realm of young wizards and various science-fiction TV shows and novels, the concept may not be that far away. A professor from the University of St Andrews in the UK is working on a sort of 'cloaking device' and researchers in California have been working on a material that can 'bend' light around 3D objects.

✓ **FACT** OR **FICTION**

148

ot all couples are able to conceive a child naturally. Sometimes, science has to step in. In 1978 the very first test-tube baby was born. Scientists had managed to fertilise the mother's egg outside the womb before replacing it. The baby was born healthy on 25 July 1978 and her name is Louise Joy Brown. Since then, many families have been made very happy thanks to the wonders of modern science.

✓ **FACT** **OR** **FICTION**

Freaky Fact or Fiction

149

Known as Q-tips in the USA and cotton buds elsewhere in the English-speaking world, these tiny little tools for cleaning out the ears or for aiding the cleaning of babies have been around since 1925. They were designed by Leo Gerstenzang from Poland. Although the sticks were originally made from wood, they were changed to the paper variety as seen in British lollipop sticks. The American name comes from 'Quick Tips'.

 ✓ FACT **OR** **FICTION**

Inventions

150

Cloning is the scientific process of duplicating a living creature to make it genetically identical to its mother. Back in 1995, Keith Campbell and Ian Wilmut, working for the Roslin Institute in Scotland, began work on cloning a sheep. The now famous 'Dolly' was born in July 1996 and was exactly like her mother. Although there may be some arguments against genetic cloning, one of the arguments for it is to help prevent endangered species like the gaur (an ox from Asia) dying out completely.

✓ **FACT** OR **FICTION**

Freaky Fact or Fiction

151

Space stations are more than just a dream of science-fiction writers. In 1973, NASA launched their Skylab space station. Its primary use was as an observation centre so information could be collected about the sun and comets. It was also used to experiment with the possibilities of manufacturing while in space. This amazing piece of technology remained in the heavens until 1979, but it certainly wasn't the last!

 FACT OR FICTION

152 Any fans of *Wonder Woman* will know about her invisible plane. How close is it to reality? Well, that's a good question. Stealth aircraft can be nearly invisible when it comes to radar. Radar can detect objects using radio waves, but if the object is shaped in a way that deflects the radio waves at a different angle, the information will not be returned to the source and so can remain undetected. In 1983, the US Lockheed F-117 was not only shaped oddly, but it was also painted with radar-absorbing paint.

 FACT **OR** **FICTION**

Freaky Fact or Fiction

153

If you know of anyone who likes a bit of DIY (Do It Yourself), you may also know that they have a faithful workbench in their shed or garage. This workbench may be a Black & Decker Workmate and it is useful on many different levels as it has various attachments including a vice. It was invented by Ron Hickman in 1968. Although it was later bought and mass-produced by Black & Decker, he originally called it the Multibench.

 ✓ FACT   OR   FICTION

154 One of life's little pleasures can be soaking in a lovely deep bath and relaxing. For an extra indulgence, it's nice to have a whirlpool bath in which little jets pump air into the water and make it bubble. This luxurious design came from the mind of Roy Jacuzzi back in 1968. During the '80s it became a highly sought luxury item for many homes around the world. Since then, the Jacuzzi company has gone on to produce a variety of bathroom appliances.

✓ **FACT**   **OR**   **FICTION**

155

The smoke alarm is a valuable installation in most homes. It was invented in 1967 by a company in the USA named BRK Electronics. The device usually fits onto the ceiling and it produces a loud beeping sound when it detects any form of smoke. This alerts the occupants of the building that there may be a fire and they can act accordingly.

✓ **FACT** **OR** **FICTION**

156

The ring pull on a can of drink was not always a standard feature. For a long time, people had to have a special can opener to be able to access the liquid inside. Ermal Fraze from Ohio, USA, began designing various new techniques to open a can in the early 1960s – some early attempts proved to be too dangerous with sharp metal bits exposed. He eventually came up with a tab that could be pulled back and tucked under to prevent any accidents. The more familiar ring pull we know today was designed by Daniel Cudzik in 1975.

 FACT **OR** **FICTION**

157

The computer mouse was invented in 1964 by Doug Engelbart to co-operate with a Graphic User Interface known as 'Windows'. He called it a mouse because the cable running between it and the computer resembled a tail. Although a substantial design, it actually took nearly 20 years before it became a standard accessory to the computer. The prototype mouse was made from some modelling clay, a marble and a few watch springs.

✓ **FACT**   **OR**   **FICTION**

158 The fashion industry is always looking for new and radical looks to sell to the public. In the 1960s, the miniskirt became hugely popular. Skirts had never been so short before! Originally seen in Paris in 1964 thanks to designer Andrè Courrèges, it was the designer Mary Quant in London who raised the hem even higher and started a mad fashion craze.

 ✓ **FACT** **OR** **FICTION**

Freaky Fact or Fiction

159

Many years ago, when we wanted to phone somebody, we had to literally dial their number, which involved dragging each number in a circular motion around the dial. This was time-consuming for those longer numbers and also frustrating if you mistakenly dialled the wrong number. Push-button phones came about in 1963 thanks to AT&T – much easier on the wrist!

✓ FACT OR FICTION

160 The disposable nappy, or diaper, was invented by American chemical engineer Victor Mills. For a long time, parents had been using cloth nappies, which had to be rewashed each time. As you can imagine, this was not a pleasant task! Vic Mills was inspired after growing tired of seeing his granddaughter's dirty nappies, so he invented a type that was cheap yet disposable. His work began in the 1950s, but the product known as Pampers became available in the early '60s.

✓ **FACT** **OR** **FICTION**

Freaky Fact or Fiction

161

These days, monorails are more often seen as a leisurely ride around theme parks, but they were initially proposed as a formal mode of transport. Like trains, their carriages run on rails, but as the name suggests, they run on one rail rather than two. The earliest form of monorail was in 1880. The monorail was first invented by Lyle Lanley and the first one was built in North Haverbrook in the USA.

✓ **FACT** **OR** **FICTION**

162

Super glue is exactly as the name suggests. It's a glue that holds things super fast! The technical name for it is cyanoacrylates and it was discovered in 1942. However, it took a few years until anyone appreciated its usefulness. Two researchers in the USA named Harry Coover and Fred Joyner realised its potential and began marketing the product as Super Glue in 1958. It was briefly called Super Joyner in honour of one of the researchers.

 ✓ FACT **OR** **FICTION**

Freaky Fact or Fiction

163 How many times have you spent a few enjoyable minutes popping the bubbles in a sheet of plastic wrapping? This strangely satisfying task is not the main purpose of bubble wrap! It was invented by Alfred Fielding and Marc Chavannes, two engineers working in the US who began marketing the product in 1960. The funny thing is, they had not originally intended it as a packing product – they were trying to design textured wallpaper!

✓ **FACT**   **OR**   **FICTION**

164 Paperclips are fairly standard in offices around the world, but where did they first come from? The basic design is known as a gem clip as it was made by the British company called 'Gem'. However, it was an American engineer named William Middlebrook who patented a machine that made them back in 1899. In France a paperclip is called *'un trombone'* – do you see the resemblance?

✓ FACT OR FICTION

Freaky Fact or Fiction

165 For a long time, sound recordings were only made on wax but this did not prove to be very durable and did not always reproduce the sounds clearly. Magnetic recordings were the next step forward, using steel wire instead of wax. Not only could this new technique record sound, it could also record data and images and led the way towards digital recording. This is all down to the Danish man, Valdemar Poulson, who began his experiments in 1898.

✓ FACT OR FICTION

166

Even such a simple thing as a pencil had to have a beginning. In 1565, a German-Swiss man named Conrad Gesner realised the mineral graphite would make a suitable writing material. However, it was important that there was an implement to store the graphite and so he placed it within a wooden holder. Although he invented this simple device, he was actually a butcher in a small village near Zurich.

✓ **FACT** **OR** **FICTION**

167

Toothpaste did not always come in a tube. For many years it came in little jars but, as you can imagine, it was a little awkward and messy trying to get it onto the toothbrush. In 1896 the Colgate Company, founded by William Colgate, introduced the tube and nozzle style of toothpaste tube. This was not the very first attempt as a dentist named Washington Sheffield tried something similar four years earlier, but it was not so successful. William Colgate was originally a maker of candles and soap!

 ✓ **FACT** **OR** **FICTION**

168 To ensure a property is secure from thieves, there are many forms of security devices and locks. One of the most famous of these is the Yale lock which was invented by an American named Linus Yale in 1861, but his original design was a variation on one his father had been working on 13 years before. However, the principle used (in which a system of pins set in a specific pattern prevents any other key to turn) is something derived from the ancient Egyptians.

✓ FACT OR FICTION

169

Package holidays were an invention by Englishman Thomas Cook back in 1841. Initially, Mr Cook sought a way to help people travel from one destination to another. The first trip he organised was from Leicester to Loughborough. He charged travellers one shilling each. Over the years, the destinations became more extravagant. The first trip he organised for profit was in 1845, a trip from Leicester to Liverpool, but by 1855 he was booking trips for people travelling to Antwerp, Brussels and Paris among other places.

✓ **FACT** **OR** **FICTION**

170 Although the practice of keeping pressurised liquids in bottles and cans happened much earlier, it wasn't until 1899 that two inventors named Helbling and Pertsch began using gases as a propellant in the can. In 1927 Erik Rotheim used chemicals as the main force and then, in the Second World War, two American scientists created an aerosol can specifically for insect repellant. Their names were Lyle Goodhue and WN Sullivan.

✓ **FACT** **OR** **FICTION**

Freaky Fact or Fiction

171

Barbie has been one of the most successful toys of all time. The woman who brought Barbie to the world was actually inspired by a similar doll she had bought while in Germany. This doll was called 'Bild Lilli' and Ruth Handler thought it would be perfect for her own daughter. She fashioned a similar doll and put it on the market in 1959. Ever since, Barbie has been selling madly in a variety of designs and with many different outfits. Ruth named Barbie after Klaus Barbie, a member of the German Gestapo or secret police.

✓ **FACT** **OR** **FICTION**

172

ir bags are life-saving cushions of air which pack tightly into a secure place in the front of a vehicle, often in the steering wheel or the dashboard. Upon impact, the bag will fill with air and stop the driver or passenger from getting any nasty bangs on the head. The prototype air bag was invented by John Hetrick from Pennsylvania, USA, in 1953. At more or less the same time, a German inventor named Walter Linderer also came up with a similar idea.

✓ **FACT** **OR** **FICTION**

173

The first Olympic Games were back in 776 BC and it has been recorded that cheesecake was one of the foods eaten by the athletes. (So it must be good for you, right?) Even though cheese has been eaten for at least 4000 years, it took a long time to perfect the cheesecake. Cream cheese wasn't invented until 1872 and James Kraft developed pasteurised cream cheese in 1880.

✓ **FACT**   **OR**   **FICTION**

174

Comic books have been a staple reading material for young and old for many years. The first known example of the modern comic book style was by a Swiss teacher named Rodolphe Töpffer (1799–1846), who would have liked to become an artist like his father, but he suffered from an eye defect so became a teacher. This did not stop him from pursuing his art, and he began telling historical stories using images and words.

 FACT **OR** **FICTION**

Freaky Fact or Fiction

175

The telescope has a long history and there are many people responsible for its invention. The facts are a little muddied in history, but what we do know is that in 1608 Hans Lippershey from the Netherlands discovered that you could make objects appear closer when looking through two separate lenses aligned together. Later, in 1609, Galileo wrote about his activities experimenting with looking at the stars with a similar device. The term 'telescope' was coined by Prince Frederick Sesi in 1611 after witnessing Galileo's work.

✓ **FACT** **OR** **FICTION**

176

The very popular board game called Trivial Pursuit was invented by two Canadians who worked for a newspaper. Scott Abbott and Chris Haney created the game around Christmas 1979 and it went on sale to the public in 1981. It soon became a global phenomenon. The game originally came about while the two men were playing a game of Murder in the Dark (quite hard with only two people) and then decided to create a trivia-based board game.

 ✓ **FACT** **OR** **FICTION**

177

A fly swat is a device used for (guess…) swatting flies! Basically, it is similar in shape to a spatula but is a little more flexible. The holes in the flat surface are there because a fly can sense the air pressure change from a solid surface, so it was best to add holes to reduce that effect. It was designed by Dr Samuel Crumbine who was infuriated by the many flies pestering him in the summer of 1905 in Kansas, USA.

✓ **FACT** ● **OR** ● **FICTION**

178 Bette Nesmith Graham was the woman who invented liquid paper. Known by various brand names, the products are essentially the same. Bette was a secretary at a bank in Texas and with the introduction of carbon-ribboned typewriters, became frustrated that mistakes were harder to correct. So, she devised a quick-drying water-based paint which could be applied with a brush. Interestingly, Bette was also the mother of Mike Nesmith, a member of the 1960s pop group The Monkees.

✓ **FACT** **OR** **FICTION**

Freaky Fact or Fiction

179

Americans Noah McVicker and his nephew Joseph McVicker were the guys behind the invention of Play-Doh. It was Joseph who figured out that a wallpaper cleaning product made by his mother's cleaning company would make good modelling clay. In 1956, Noah and Joseph began the Rainbow Crafts Company and mass-produced the colourful clay. Although Play-Doh was initially an off-white colour, the McVickers soon supplied different colours, including red, blue, green and tartan.

✓ FACT OR FICTION

180

Cling film or cling wrap is a plastic wrapping that is similar to PVC. It was invented by a man named Ralph Wiley while he was working for the Dow Chemical Company. Originally it was made from Saran polyvinylidene chloride (try saying that quickly!) and so he named it Saran wrap. It was used initially as a water-proof covering for planes during World War II and it was green and smelled pretty disgusting. Since then, the colour was removed (and the smell!) and it was deemed suitable for food preparation.

 FACT **OR** **FICTION**

181

Liposuction is a form of cosmetic surgery in which the loose fat on the body can be removed by a machine which sucks the fat out of the flesh. It was invented by Dr Giorgio Fischer, an Italian doctor who founded the International Academy of Cosmetic Surgery. The term comes from the Greek word '*Lipos*', which means 'fat'.

 FACT   **OR**   **FICTION**

182

Barbed wire was invented by Joseph F Glidden from Illinois, USA. Although there were other forms of wire fences used by farmers across America, a lot of the designs were expensive to produce. Glidden's design was the cheapest to reproduce but he was also up against a lot of copycats who tried to steal the rights to his idea. However, after three years of legal battles, the claim was all his.

✓ **FACT** **OR** **FICTION**

183 Esperanto is a relatively new language that was invented by Ludwik Zamenhof in 1887. He was inspired to do so because of the problems caused by so many different languages not interacting with each other. A number of other 'universal' languages have been attempted, but this is one that seemed to catch on – at least in the 1970s when it was popular. The only problem is finding someone else who speaks it these days is rather difficult.

 ✓ **FACT** **OR** **FICTION**

184

Early versions of the submarine date back as far as 1620 when a Dutchman named Cornelis Drebbel built a submersible boat. The boat made a few trips along the Thames in London and one of the passengers was King James I. The more modern version of the submarine was pursued by the US military and a variety of prototypes were made during the following centuries. Two early designs were called the Platypus and the Toad.

 ✓ **FACT** **OR** **FICTION**

185

The first skyscraper built with a steel frame was in Chicago, Illinois, USA, in 1885. The architect was William Le Baron Jenney. Sadly this revolutionary building was demolished in the 1930s. The term 'skyscraper' actually comes from 13th-century Italy when buildings that were a mere 91.4 m (300 ft) tall were considered to scrape the sky.

✓ FACT OR FICTION

186 Frisbees were one of those inventions that happened due to the need for play! William Russell Frisbie had his own baking company in the 1870s in Connecticut, USA, and he baked a lot of pies. The pies were baked in shallow pie tins which had his name embossed into the underside. These pie dishes, once empty, were quite aero-dynamic and it wasn't long before people were throwing them around in a game of catch.

✓ **FACT** OR **FICTION**

We use tongs in kitchens on a regular basis, especially when frying or grilling food. They can come in different shapes but they all have the same basic function – to help cooks handle hot food without getting burned. Blacksmiths also use a larger form of tongs when handling hot metal. There is evidence to suggest that tongs have been around for a few thousand years in some form or other, as seen in Egyptian wall paintings!

 ✓ **FACT** OR **FICTION**

188 **P**rozac is a drug that helps to fight depression. It was invented by Ray Fuller and a team of scientists in 1972, though it took a further 15 years to develop into the common prescription drug. It is a Selective Serotonin Reuptake Inhibitor drug, which basically means it blocks the part of the brain that causes depression. Although it does have a reasonable success rate, there are instances of a chemical upset in the brain causing varied mood swings.

✓ **FACT** **OR** **FICTION**

Freaky Fact or Fiction

189

Ruth Wakefield is the woman we have to thank for inventing the chocolate chip cookie! She was born in 1905 and eventually opened a little inn (called the Toll House Inn) with her husband. In 1930 she was making cookies and ran out of cooking chocolate, so decided to substitute some Nestlé eating chocolate. However, when they went in the oven the chocolate in the cookies didn't melt. Instead of being a disaster, these new cookies were simply delicious. The staff at Nestlé were so happy when their chocolate sales increased, they made a bronze statue of Ruth Wakefield.

 ✓ **FACT** **OR** **FICTION**

190 Margarine was invented in 1870 by a Frenchman named Hippolyte Mège-Mouriez after the Emperor Louis Napoleon III asked for someone to come up with a suitable substitute for butter. Hippolyte's product was the most successful entry in the competition and although the recipe has changed over the years, it has always had the same name. Hippolyte named it after his wife, Marguerite.

✓ **FACT** **OR** **FICTION**

Freaky Fact or Fiction

191

Gunpowder has been around since the end of the 9th century or even earlier. It is a mixture of sulfur, charcoal and potassium nitrate. Mixed in the right quantities, it can be rather explosive. Although we tend to think of gunpowder as the substance used in guns or for explosions such as Guy Fawkes' ill-fated attempt to blow up the British Parliament, its original use was for fireworks in China.

 FACT **OR** **FICTION**

192 Make-up is an important part of life for many people. It is used professionally by performers on stage or film, but more commonly as a beauty product. Although various types of lipstick have been around for hundreds of years, the lipstick tube was an idea by Maurice Levy in 1915. He realised it would be more convenient for women to carry around, be easier to apply to the face and would also protect the contents of a woman's handbag from being covered in lipstick if the cosmetic was housed in a tube.

✓ **FACT** OR **FICTION**

193

Perspex originally came from a German company named Röhm & Haas, which was making a form of plexiglass back in the early 1930s. A later extension of this acrylic plastic was created by Rowland Hill and John Crawford from Britain. Around the same time, an American company called DuPont had a similar product called 'Lucite'.

✓ **FACT**   **OR**   **FICTION**

194

Penny Farthing was a keen young inventor who wanted to make a mode of transport that would get her around town easily. She invented a bicycle with a large front wheel and a small rear wheel which, although a little difficult to board, was easy to control. The large wheel was 1.5 m (60 in) in diameter (sometimes more!). It was eventually named after the inventor.

✓ FACT OR FICTION

195

The SeaCat is a wave-piercing catamaran which is capable of terrific speeds through the water. It was designed and built by two men, Robert Clifford and Philip Hercus, who later were awarded the Order of Australia (the AO) in 1995. Originally, the boats were designed for trips to the Antarctic.

✓ **FACT**   **OR**   **FICTION**

196

The electric toothbrush was invented in 1954 by a dentist named Phillipe Guy Woog. He also invented a number of other dental tools. The toothbrush was called the Broxodent and it had a movable head which would rotate thanks to a motor within the handle. Woog also invented the electric power drill, inspired by his own toothbrush.

✓ **FACT**   **OR**   **FICTION**

197

The jukebox was invented by Louis Glass and William Arnold in 1889. Basically, this machine was a coin-operated phonograph with four 'listening tubes' for customers to use as it didn't blast out the sound through speakers. However, the term 'jukebox' did not become the favoured name until the 1930s, when it was a nickname thought up in the southern states of the USA. There is debate about the origin of the nickname, but it may come from the African word 'jook', meaning 'wicked'.

 ✓ **FACT** **OR** **FICTION**

198 ary Anderson was born in Alabama, USA. In 1903, she was disturbed when she noticed that streetcar drivers had to lean out of their windows when the weather was bad in order to see. So, with this in mind, Anderson invented the windshield wiper. Although they now work automatically, powered by the engine, the first wipers were moved by a lever inside the streetcar.

✓ **FACT** OR **FICTION**

Freaky Fact or Fiction

199

The jock strap is not merely a type of underwear. It was actually specifically designed for the athlete to wear as a comfortable undergarment. It was invented by Joe Cartledge, the founder of the Guelph Elastic Hosiery Company, in 1920 and was originally called Protex. Interestingly, an inventor from Finland named Parvo Nakacheker claims that he designed the jock strap first.

✓ **FACT**   **OR**   **FICTION**

200 Electric washing machines were invented in the early 20th century. Alva Fisher from Chicago, Illinois, was one of the first to develop an electric washing machine, filing the patent on 27 May 1909. Clothes had been washed in a variety of ways before this, and included the use of washboards, mangles and the old faithful rock by a stream! This new machine was basically a drum cylinder with holes in it spinning around in a tub of water. It would do a number of turns in one direction and then again in the opposite direction. It was powered by a foot pedal like the old sewing machines.

✓ **FACT** **OR** **FICTION**

201

Nail polish has two purposes. Firstly, it actually can protect the nail. Secondly, it adds a fashionable touch to the hand. The painting of nails dates back thousands of years. Chinese royalty would paint their nails, but there has also been evidence of the ancient Egyptians doing the same thing. In more modern times, we see more variety of colour in the ink and sometimes even glitter.

 ✓ **FACT** OR **FICTION**

Inventions

202

Blissymbols are a collection of images representing words. The system was created in the mid-1970s by Charles Bliss who wanted to find a way of mass communication. In the mid-'80s, a 12-year-old Canadian girl named Rachel Zimmerman developed a new software program that could help non-speaking people to communicate, translating the Blissymbols into words. In 1985, Zimmerman won a silver medal for her invention at the Canada-wide World Exhibition of Achievement of Young Inventors.

✓ **FACT** **OR** **FICTION**

Freaky Fact or Fiction

203

Scotchguard is a product designed to cover fabrics and make them more resistant to spills and stains. It was invented by accident one day in a laboratory. Patsy Sherman and Sam Smith were working on developing fluorochemicals. When some accidentally fell onto an assistant's shoes, they were astonished to find that the substance was practically invisible, but was still difficult to remove as it repelled water. This led to their discovery of the fabric coating, which has been in production since the late 1950s.

 ✓ FACT OR FICTION

204

Movies have come a long way since their origins. These days we can see full-colour spectacles with lots of special effects and sometimes even 3D. However, for a while, movies were silent, and black and white only. The first 'Talking Picture' was *The Jazz Singer* starring Al Jolson, which was made in the US in 1927. It wasn't the first to incorporate sound, but it was the first to feature dialogue. The first British movie to feature sound dialogue was Alfred Hitchcock's *The Lodger*.

 FACT **OR** **FICTION**

Answers

1. This is, sadly, **fiction**! However, Thomas Crapper was a plumber and during the 1860s he started a business entitled 'Thomas Crapper & Co.', which provided sanitary lavatory plumbing indoors for homes.

2. Fact.

3. Fact.

4. Fiction. A DuPont chemist named Stephanie Kwolek discovered the super-strong fibre in 1965. This led to the development of Kevlar, which was patented in 1971.

5. Fact.

6. Fact.

7. Fact.

8. Fiction. Thomas Edison's recorded words were 'Mary had a little lamb'.

9. Fact.

10. Fact.

11. Fiction. Although Daisuke Inoue did invent the first karaoke machine in the 1970s, the word karaoke is actually made up from two Japanese words which mean 'empty' and 'orchestra'.

12. Fact.

13. Fiction. Wilhelm Röntgen may have invented the X-ray, but X-ray Specs are merely a comic book fantasy... so far.

14. Fact.

15. Fiction. Scratch and sniff iPods are not currently planned.

16. Fact.

17. Fact.

18. Fiction. The first two commercially released compact discs were Abba's *The Visitors* and Richard Strauss's *An Alpine Symphony*.

19. Fact.

20. Fact.

21. Fact.

22. Fact, although similar bear toys were also being produced in Germany by Margarete Steiff, whose bear designs are the ones we are more familiar with today.

23. Fact.

24. Fiction. The polygraph measures various things, including the wearer's pulse, blood pressure, breathing rate and sweatiness.

25. Fact.

26. Fact.

27. Fact.

28. Fact.

29. Fact.

30. Fact.

31. Fact.

32. Fiction. It was not a yeast-based liquid in the tube. It was mercury, the liquid chemical element.

33. Fiction. The words 'plastic', 'snorkel' and 'bling' were words invented in the 20th century.

34. Fiction. 'The Loco-motion' became popular in the 1960s thanks to a song of the same name performed by American singer Little Eva. It had a comeback in the 1980s when it was covered by Australian Kylie Minogue.

35. Fact.

36. Fact.

37. Fact.

38. Fiction. The correct signal for SOS in Morse code is Dot Dot Dot, Dash Dash Dash, Dot Dot Dot.

39. Fact.

40. Fiction. The first stamp was called the Penny Black, as it cost just a penny to post a letter.

41. Fact.

42. Fact.

43. Fact.

44. Fact.

45. Fact.

46. Fact.

47. Fact.

48. Fiction. There is no rubber in bubble gum, thankfully.

49. Fact.

50. Fact.

51. Fact.

52. Fact.

53. Mostly fact, except for the pretty colours and designs!

54. Fiction. It certainly wasn't nitrous oxide. That's laughing gas!

55. Fact.

56. Fiction. Dunlop did not work in a circus. He was a vet.

Answers

57. All fact, except for the image William Friese-Greene recorded. That is fiction. The first images were of passers-by and horse-drawn carriages on Hyde Park corner, London. There was not a custard pie to be seen – sadly.

58. Fact.

59. Fact. Gabor Hall is named after the inventor of holography.

60. Fact.

61. Fact.

62. Fact.

63. Fact.

64. Fact.

65. Fiction. Oddly enough, the two brothers who invented the machine did not test it themselves.

66. Fact.

67. Fact.

68. Fiction. A cyclotron is a particle accelerator that irradiates biological matter and can make things radioactive. This is useful in the study of physics and ultimately provides therapeutic remedies for the body, among other things.

69. Fact.

70. Fact.

71. Fact.

72. Fact.

73. Fact.

74. Fact.

75. Fiction. Although the slide raft is a part of most aircraft's safety gear, they are not featured on trains or buses.

76. Fiction. The origin of the word 'pogo' is debatable, but it certainly does not stand for 'Pounce On, Go Orbital'!

77. Fiction. The escalator was exhibited in Paris, but not in 1950. It was half a century earlier, in 1900!

78. Fact.

79. Fact.

80. Fact.

81. Fact.

82. Fiction. There is no kiwi fruit in the polish.

83. Fact.

84. Fact.

85. Fact. The exact nature of the discovery is not (and may never be) known, but Maria Ann Smith was the woman who discovered them.

86. Fact.

87. Fiction. Dr David Vickers did create some microsurgery instruments, but not mini-robots.

88. Fact.

89. Fact.

90. Fiction. SOLA stands for Scientific Optical Laboratories of Australia.

91. Fact.

92. Fiction. The bandaid has been available since 1921, not 1721.

93. Fact.

94. Fiction. The first winner completed the race in 44 hours.

95. Fact.

96. Fact.

97. Fiction. The first razors were made out of brass and sheet steel.

98. Fact.

99. Fiction. Saunders' chain was called 'Piggly Wiggly'.

100. Fact. The tank was indeed nicknamed 'Little Willie'.

101. Fact.

102. Fact

103. Fact.

104. Fact.

105. Fiction. Although Percy Shaw didn't become Prime Minister of England, James Callaghan did (from 1976 to 1979). However, many years before his successful election, while working for the Ministry of Transport, Callaghan was responsible for buying millions of Shaw's cat's eyes and implementing them in roads around England.

106. Fact.

107. Fiction. The parking meter was invented by Carl Magee, but he wasn't a traffic warden. He was a newspaper editor.

108. Fact.

Answers

109. Fact.

110. Fiction. Roy Plunkett discovered this new plastic by accident while he was trying to discover a new non-toxic refrigerant gas. Nor did he work for NASA; he worked as a chemist.

111. Fact.

112. Fact.

113. Fact.

114. Fact.

115. Fiction. It's all true, except for it being named after their pet snake. Betty James thought the word 'Slinky' best suited its slithering nature.

116. Fact.

117. Fact.

118. Fact.

119. Fact.

120. Fact.

121. Fiction. There are no custard beds.

122. Fact.

123. Fact.

124. Fact.

125. Fiction. The designer was called Erno Rubik, hence the name 'Rubik's Cube'.

126. Fiction. Although Eli Whitney did invent the cotton gin, it did not bring him great wealth. As it was such a simple device, many copied it and his company went out of business.

127. Fiction. The Anderson Shelters were merely named after the man in government who issued the shelters. Sir John Anderson was Home Secretary at the time.

128. Fact.

129. Fact.

130. Fact.

131. Fiction. Strangely, sales were not high initially. Elisha Otis only sold three elevators in the first year. It wasn't until a few years later that sales started to rise.

132. Fact.

133. Fact.

134. Fiction. Dr Banting and his student, Charles Best, did indeed figure out the best source of insulin, but it was not from any tree! It was from the pancreas of certain animals, and Banting and

Best discovered how to extract it without it being destroyed by the gland's digestive juices. Today, the majority of insulin used by diabetics is a form of human insulin made using DNA technology.

135. Fact.

136. Fiction. Sadly, Mr Higinbotham did not become a millionaire as he did not patent his creation. In 1972 a man named Nolan Bushnell patented 'Pong', which was very similar to Higinbotham's game.

137. Fiction. The first crime solved was a murder back in January 1987.

138. Fact.

139. Fact.

140. Fact.

141. Fact.

142. Fiction. Before the miners had the rail system, they had to carry all the rocks and minerals by hand or in bumpy carts.

143. Fact.

144. Fact.

145. Fact.

146. Fact. The name 'tarmac' comes from the words 'Tar' and 'Macadam', the latter being a term for road construction pioneered by John McAdam from Scotland.

147. Fact. Richard Schowengerdt of California has already patented his own Cloaking System with the US Patent office, patent # US5307162.

148. Fact.

149. Fiction. The Q in 'Q-tip' stands for Quality.

150. Fact.

151. Fact.

152. Fact.

153. Fiction. Ron Hickman's invention was the Minibench, not the Multibench.

154. Fact.

155. Fact.

156. Fact.

157. Fiction. The first mouse was actually made of wood with two metal wheels.

158. Fact.

Answers

159. Fact.

160. Fact.

161. Fiction. Lyle Lanley did not invent the monorail. He was a character in the animated TV series *The Simpsons,* created by Matt Groening. German engineer Eugen Langen built the first successful monorail in 1901 and it still runs in Wuppertal, North-West Germany.

162. Fiction. It was never called Super Joyner.

163. Fact. But we can see why they opted for the packaging!

164. Fact.

165. Fact.

166. Fiction. Although Gesner did design the pencil, he was not a butcher. He was a professor in ethics, physics and natural sciences, and worked in medicine.

167. Fact.

168. Fact.

169. Fact.

170. Fact.

171. Fiction. Barbie was named after the creator's daughter, Barbara. The doll's full name is Barbara Millicent Roberts.

172. Fact.

173. Fact.

174. Fact.

175. Fact.

176. Fiction. The two inventors were inspired while playing a game of Scrabble.

177. Fact.

178. Fact.

179. Fiction. A tartan-coloured Play-Doh would not stay tartan for long!

180. Fact.

181. Fact.

182. Fact.

183. Fact.

184. Fiction. Two early designs of submarine were named the Turtle in 1775 and the Alligator in 1863 – both proved to be unsuccessful.

185. Fact.

186. Fact. Apparently, the pie-tin throwing game was popular with students at Yale University in the 1940s.

187. Fact.

188. Fact.

189. Fiction. She was given a lifetime supply of Nestlé chocolate!

190. Fiction. The name 'margarine' was inspired by the margaric acid used in the making of the spread. Margaric acid is so called because it resembles pearls and the Greek word for pearl is '*margarites*'.

191. Fact.

192. Fact.

193. Fact.

194. Fiction. The Penny Farthing was invented by James Starley and William Hillman in the late 19th century. It was named after the two coins of differing sizes then in use in Britain, the penny and the farthing, which the wheels resembled.

195. Fiction. The boats were initially designed for trips to the Great Barrier Reef off the northeastern coast of Australia.

196. Fiction. The electric power drill was invented by Wilhelm Fein in 1895.

197. Fact.

198. Fact.

199. Fact.

200. Fiction. It was powered by an electric motor.

201. Fact.

202. Fact.

203. Fact.

204. Fiction. The first British film to feature sound dialogue was not *The Lodger*. It was *Blackmail* in 1929, but it certainly was directed by Alfred Hitchcock.

Sources

1. Roger Bridgman, *1000 Inventions & Discoveries* (book), 2006; Thomas Crapper & Co Ltd, www.thomas-crapper.com, 2009

2. *Encyclopaedia Britannica*, 2005

3. Encyclopaedia Britannica Online, www.britannica.com, 2010

4. Roger Bridgman, *1000 Inventions & Discoveries* (book), 2006

5. *Encyclopaedia Britannica*, 2005

6. *Encyclopaedia Britannica*, 2005

7. *Encyclopaedia Britannica*, 2005

8. *Encyclopaedia Britannica*, 2005; Project Gutenberg, www.gutenberg.org, 2010

9. *Encyclopaedia Britannica*, 2005; Madeau Stewart, *The Music Lover's Guide to the Instruments of the Orchestra* (book), 1980

10. Encyclopaedia Britannica Online, www.britannica.com, 2010

11. 'Daisuke Inoue', *Time Asia* (magazine), August 1999

12. Roger Bridgman, *1000 Inventions & Discoveries* (book), 2006

13. *Encyclopaedia Britannica*, 2005

14. *Encyclopaedia Britannica*, 2005

15. Roger Bridgman, *1000 Inventions & Discoveries* (book), 2006

16. Roger Bridgman, *1000 Inventions & Discoveries* (book), 2006

17. Iridium Satellite Communications, www.iridium.com, 2010

18. 'How the CD was developed', BBC News, http://news.bbc.co.uk, 2007

19. Margaret McPhee, *The Dictionary of Australian Inventions and Discoveries* (book), 1993

20. Roger Bridgman, *1000 Inventions & Discoveries* (book), 2006

21. *The Biographical Dictionary of Scientists: Vol. 6; Engineers & Inventors*, 1985

22. Roger Bridgman, *1000 Inventions & Discoveries* (book), 2006

23. Roger Bridgman, *1000 Inventions & Discoveries* (book), 2006

24. Roger Bridgman, *1000 Inventions & Discoveries* (book), 2006

25. *Encyclopaedia Britannica*, 2005

26. 'How to do Venn Diagram Problems', eHow, www.ehow.com, 2010

27. *Encyclopaedia Britannica*, 2005

28. *Encyclopaedia Britannica*, 2005

29. English-Wine.com, www.english-wine.com, 2001

30. Roger Bridgman, *1000 Inventions & Discoveries* (book), 2006

31. Roger Bridgman, *1000 Inventions & Discoveries* (book), 2006

32. *Encyclopaedia Britannica*, 2005

33. Roger Bridgman, *1000 Inventions & Discoveries* (book), 2006; David Crystal, *Dr Johnson's Dictionary: An Anthology* (book), 2005

34. *Encyclopaedia Britannica*, 2005

35. Roger Bridgman, *1000 Inventions & Discoveries* (book), 2006

36. *Encyclopaedia Britannica*, 2005; C Michael Mellor, *Louis Braille: A Touch of Genius* (book), 2006

37. Roger Bridgman, *1000 Inventions & Discoveries* (book), 2006

38. *Encyclopaedia Britannica*, 2005

39. Roger Bridgman, *1000 Inventions & Discoveries* (book), 2006

40. *Encyclopaedia Britannica*, 2005

41. Roger Bridgman, *1000 Inventions & Discoveries* (book), 2006

42. *Encyclopaedia Britannica*, 2005

43. Margaret McPhee, *The Dictionary of Australian Inventions and Discoveries* (book), 1993

44. *Encyclopaedia Britannica*, 2005; 'The Holy War on SUVs', Forbes.com, www.forbes.com, 2003

45. *Margaret McPhee, The Dictionary of Australian Inventions and Discoveries* (book), 1993; Powerhouse Museum, www.powerhousemuseum.com, 2001

46. *Encyclopaedia Britannica*, 2005; Roger Bridgman, *1000 Inventions & Discoveries* (book), 2006

47. Roger Bridgman, *1000 Inventions & Discoveries* (book), 2006; Absolute Astronomy, www.absoluteastronomy.com, 2010; Encyclopaedia Britannica Online, www.britannica.com, 2010

48. Roger Bridgman, *1000 Inventions & Discoveries* (book), 2006

49. Roger Bridgman, *1000 Inventions & Discoveries* (book), 2006

50. *The Biographical Dictionary of Scientists: Vol. 6; Engineers & Inventors*, 1985

51. *The Biographical Dictionary of Scientists: Vol. 6; Engineers & Inventors*, 1985

52. *The Biographical Dictionary of Scientists: Vol. 6; Engineers & Inventors*, 1985

53. *The Biographical Dictionary of Scientists: Vol. 6; Engineers & Inventors*, 1985

54. *The Biographical Dictionary of Scientists: Vol. 6; Engineers & Inventors*, 1985

55. Roger Bridgman, *1000 Inventions & Discoveries* (book), 2006; Nottinghamshire History, www.nottshistory.org.uk, 2003

56. *The Biographical Dictionary of Scientists: Vol. 6; Engineers & Inventors*, 1985

57. *The Biographical Dictionary of Scientists: Vol. 6; Engineers & Inventors*, 1985; Screen Online, www.screenonline.org.uk, 2010

58. Kodak, www.kodak.com, 2010

59. *The Biographical Dictionary of Scientists: Vol. 6; Engineers & Inventors*, 1985

60. *The Biographical Dictionary of Scientists: Vol. 6; Engineers & Inventors*, 1985

61. Margaret McPhee, *The Dictionary of Australian Inventions and Discoveries* (book), 1993

62. *The Biographical Dictionary of Scientists: Vol. 6; Engineers & Inventors*, 1985

63. *The Biographical Dictionary of Scientists: Vol. 6; Engineers & Inventors*, 1985

64. *The Biographical Dictionary of Scientists: Vol. 6; Engineers & Inventors*, 1985

65. *The Biographical Dictionary of Scientists: Vol. 6; Engineers & Inventors*, 1985

66. *The Biographical Dictionary of Scientists: Vol. 6; Engineers & Inventors*, 1985

67. *The Biographical Dictionary of Scientists: Vol. 6; Engineers & Inventors*, 1985

68. *The World Book Encyclopaedia of Science: Vol. 8; Men and Women of Science*

69. *The World Book Encyclopaedia of Science: Vol. 8; Men and Women of Science;* Stephen Van Dulken, *Inventing the 20th Century: 100 Inventions that Shaped the World* (book), 2002

Sources

70. Stephen Van Dulken, *Inventing the 20th Century: 100 Inventions that Shaped the World* (book), 2002

71. Margaret McPhee, *The Dictionary of Australian Inventions and Discoveries* (book), 1993

72. United States Patent and Tradesmark Office, www.uspto.gov, 2009; American Heritage, www.americanheritage.com, 2005

73. Hasbro, www.hasbro.com, 2008; The Art of Murder, www.theartofmurder.com, 2010

74. Dr Peter Mark Roget, *Roget's Thesaurus* (book), 2002; Encyclopaedia Britannica Online, www.britannica.com, 2010

75. Margaret McPhee, *The Dictionary of Australian Inventions and Discoveries* (book), 1993

76. American Pogo Stick Company, www.pogostickusa.com, 2005

77. Roger Bridgman, *1000 Inventions & Discoveries* (book), 2006

78. Margaret McPhee, *The Dictionary of Australian Inventions and Discoveries* (book), 1993

79. 3M, www.3m.com, 2010

80. Margaret McPhee, *The Dictionary of Australian Inventions and Discoveries* (book), 1993; The Bionic Ear Institute, www.bionicear.org, 2010; Cochlear, www.cochlear.com, 2010

81. *The Biographical Dictionary of Scientists: Vol. 6; Engineers & Inventors*, 1985

82. Margaret McPhee, *The Dictionary of Australian Inventions and Discoveries* (book), 1993

83. Roger Bridgman, *1000 Inventions & Discoveries* (book), 2006

84. Margaret McPhee, *The Dictionary of Australian Inventions and Discoveries* (book), 1993

85. Margaret McPhee, *The Dictionary of Australian Inventions and Discoveries* (book), 1993

86. Margaret McPhee, *The Dictionary of Australian Inventions and Discoveries* (book), 1993; *Encyclopaedia Britannica*, 1983; PubMed Central, www.ncbi.nlm.nih.gov/pmc, 2006

87. Margaret McPhee, *The Dictionary of Australian Inventions and Discoveries* (book), 1993; Microsurgeon.org, www.microsurgeon.org, 2010

88. Margaret McPhee, *The Dictionary of Australian Inventions and Discoveries* (book), 1993; Mike Croll, *The History of Landmines* (book) 1998

89. Margaret McPhee, *The Dictionary of Australian Inventions and Discoveries* (book), 1993; Stephen Van Dulken, *Inventing the 20th Century: 100 Inventions that Shaped the World* (book), 2002; Heart Rhythm Society, www.hrsonline.org, 1998

90. Margaret McPhee, *The Dictionary of Australian Inventions and Discoveries* (book), 1993

91. Margaret McPhee, *The Dictionary of Australian Inventions and Discoveries* (book), 1993

92. Johnson & Johnson, www.jnj.com, 2010

93. Margaret McPhee, *The Dictionary of Australian Inventions and Discoveries* (book), 1993

94. Margaret McPhee, *The Dictionary of Australian Inventions and Discoveries* (book), 1993; Solar Powered Cars, www.solarpoweredcars.net, 2010; Global Green Challenge, www.globalgreenchallenge.com.au, 2010

95. *Encyclopaedia Britannica*, 2005

96. Stephen Van Dulken, *Inventing the 20th Century: 100 Inventions that Shaped the World* (book), 2002

97. Stephen Van Dulken, *Inventing the 20th Century: 100 Inventions that Shaped the World* (book), 2002

98. Stephen Van Dulken, *Inventing the 20th Century: 100 Inventions that Shaped the World* (book), 2002

Sources

99. Stephen Van Dulken, *Inventing the 20th Century: 100 Inventions that Shaped the World* (book), 2002

100. HP Willmott, *World War I* (book), 2003

101. Stephen Van Dulken, *Inventing the 20th Century: 100 Inventions that Shaped the World* (book), 2002

102. Stephen Van Dulken, *Inventing the 20th Century: 100 Inventions that Shaped the World* (book), 2002

103. Stephen Van Dulken, *Inventing the 20th Century: 100 Inventions that Shaped the World* (book), 2002

104. Stephen Van Dulken, *Inventing the 20th Century: 100 Inventions that Shaped the World* (book), 2002

105. Stephen Van Dulken, *Inventing the 20th Century: 100 Inventions that Shaped the World* (book), 2002

106. Stephen Van Dulken, *Inventing the 20th Century: 100 Inventions that Shaped the World* (book), 2002

107. Stephen Van Dulken, *Inventing the 20th Century: 100 Inventions that Shaped the World* (book), 2002

108. Stephen Van Dulken, *Inventing the 20th Century: 100 Inventions that Shaped the World* (book), 2002

109. Stephen Van Dulken, *Inventing the 20th Century: 100 Inventions that Shaped the World* (book), 2002

110. Stephen Van Dulken, *Inventing the 20th Century: 100 Inventions that Shaped the World* (book), 2002

111. Stephen Van Dulken, *Inventing the 20th Century: 100 Inventions that Shaped the World* (book), 2002

112. Stephen Van Dulken, *Inventing the 20th Century: 100 Inventions that Shaped the World* (book), 2002

113. Stephen Van Dulken, *Inventing the 20th Century: 100 Inventions that Shaped the World* (book), 2002

114. Stephen Van Dulken, *Inventing the 20th Century: 100 Inventions that Shaped the World* (book), 2002

115. Stephen Van Dulken, *Inventing the 20th Century: 100 Inventions that Shaped the World* (book), 2002

116. Stephen Van Dulken, *Inventing the 20th Century: 100 Inventions that Shaped the World* (book), 2002

117. Stephen Van Dulken, *Inventing the 20th Century: 100 Inventions that Shaped the World* (book), 2002

118. Stephen Van Dulken, *Inventing the 20th Century: 100 Inventions that Shaped the World* (book), 2002

119. Stephen Van Dulken, *Inventing the 20th Century: 100 Inventions that Shaped the World* (book), 2002

120. Stephen Van Dulken, *Inventing the 20th Century: 100 Inventions that Shaped the World* (book), 2002

121. Stephen Van Dulken, *Inventing the 20th Century: 100 Inventions that Shaped the World* (book), 2002

122. Stephen Van Dulken, *Inventing the 20th Century: 100 Inventions that Shaped the World* (book), 2002

123. ABC Queensland, www.abc.net.au/queensland, 2005

124. Footy-boots.com, www.footyboots.com, 2010; Talk Football, www.talkfootball.co.uk, 2009

125. Stephen Van Dulken, *Inventing the 20th Century: 100 Inventions that Shaped the World* (book), 2002

126. Roger Bridgman, *1000 Inventions & Discoveries* (book), 2006

127. *World War II Day by Day* (book), 2004

128. Roger Bridgman, *1000 Inventions & Discoveries* (book), 2006

129. 'A History of the Piano from 1709 to 1980', UK Piano, www.uk-piano.org, 2010

130. Roger Bridgman, *1000 Inventions & Discoveries* (book), 2006

131. Otis Worldwide, www.otisworldwide.com, 2010

132. Roger Bridgman, *1000 Inventions & Discoveries* (book), 2006

133. Roger Bridgman, *1000 Inventions & Discoveries* (book), 2006

134. Roger Bridgman, *1000 Inventions & Discoveries* (book), 2006

135. Theremin World, www.thereminworld.com, 2009

136. Stephen Van Dulken, *Inventing the 20th Century: 100 Inventions that Shaped the World* (book), 2002

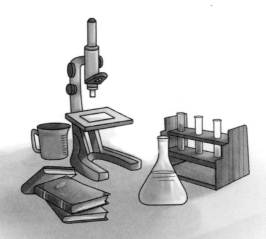

Sources

137. Stephen Van Dulken, *Inventing the 20th Century: 100 Inventions that Shaped the World* (book), 2002

138. Stephen Van Dulken, *Inventing the 20th Century: 100 Inventions that Shaped the World* (book), 2002

139. Stephen Van Dulken, *Inventing the 20th Century: 100 Inventions that Shaped the World* (book), 2002

140. Stephen Van Dulken, *Inventing the 20th Century: 100 Inventions that Shaped the World* (book), 2002

141. Roger Bridgman, *1000 Inventions & Discoveries* (book), 2006

142. Roger Bridgman, *1000 Inventions & Discoveries* (book), 2006

143. Roger Bridgman, *1000 Inventions & Discoveries* (book), 2006

144. Roger Bridgman, *1000 Inventions & Discoveries* (book), 2006

145. Stephen Van Dulken, *Inventing the 20th Century: 100 Inventions that Shaped the World* (book), 2002

146. Stephen Van Dulken, *Inventing the 20th Century: 100 Inventions that Shaped the World* (book), 2002

147. 'We Have the Technology!', *Torchwood Magazine* (magazine), UK, May/June 2010; Boliven Patents, www.boliven.com, 2010

148. Roger Bridgman, *1000 Inventions & Discoveries* (book), 2006; 'On this Day, 25 July', BBC news, http://news.bbc.co.uk, 2008

149. Roger Bridgman, *1000 Inventions & Discoveries* (book), 2006; Enchanted Learning, www.enchantedlearning.com, 2010

150. Stephen Van Dulken, *Inventing the 20th Century: 100 Inventions that Shaped the World* (book) 2002; Roger Bridgman, *1000 Inventions & Discoveries* (book), 2006

151. Roger Bridgman, *1000 Inventions & Discoveries* (book), 2006

152. Roger Bridgman, *1000 Inventions & Discoveries* (book), 2006

153. Roger Bridgman, *1000 Inventions & Discoveries* (book), 2006

154. Jacuzzi, www.jacuzzi.com, 2010; Roger Bridgman, *1000 Inventions & Discoveries* (book), 2006

155. Roger Bridgman, *1000 Inventions & Discoveries* (book), 2006

156. Ohio History Central, www.ohiohistorycentral.org, 2010; Vestal Design, www.vestaldesign.com, 2006

157. About.com, http://inventors.about.com, 2010; Roger Bridgman, *1000 Inventions & Discoveries* (book), 2006

158. Roger Bridgman, *1000 Inventions & Discoveries* (book), 2006

159. Roger Bridgman, *1000 Inventions & Discoveries* (book), 2006

160. Pampers, www.pampers.com, 2010; Roger Bridgman, *1000 Inventions & Discoveries* (book), 2006

161. Roger Bridgman, *1000 Inventions & Discoveries* (book), 2006

162. The Original Super Glue Corporation, www.supergluecorp.com, 2010

163. Roger Bridgman, *1000 Inventions & Discoveries* (book), 2006

164. Roger Bridgman, *1000 Inventions & Discoveries* (book), 2006

165. Roger Bridgman, *1000 Inventions & Discoveries* (book), 2006

166. Art Directory, www.conrad-gessner.com; Roger Bridgman, *1000 Inventions & Discoveries* (book), 2006

167. Roger Bridgman, *1000 Inventions & Discoveries* (book), 2006

168. Roger Bridgman, *1000 Inventions & Discoveries* (book), 2006

169. Thomas Cook, www.thomascook.com, 2010

170. About Aerosols, www.aboutaerosols.com, 2008

171. Barbie, www.barbiemedia.com, 2010

172. Consumer Affairs, www.consumeraffairs.com, 2006

173. Passionate About Food, www.passionateaboutfood.net, 2001

174. Lambiek, www.lambiek.net, 2009

175. 'An early history of the telescope', Antique Telescopes, www.antiquetelescopes.org; Roger Bridgman, *1000 Inventions & Discoveries* (book), 2006

176. The Great Idea Finder, www.ideafinder.com, 2005

177. 'Fly Swatter', Spiritus Temporis, www.spiritus-temporis.com, 2005

178. Famous Women Inventors, www.women-inventors.com, 2008

179. 'Play-Doh', Ohio History Central, www.ohiohistorycentral.org, 2010

180. Gourmet Britain, www.gourmetbritain.com, 2010; Roger Bridgman, *1000 Inventions & Discoveries* (book), 2006

181. European Society of Aesthetic Surgery, www.eusas.com, 2007

182. Devil's Rope Museum, www.barbwiremuseum.com, 2007; Roger Bridgman, *1000 Inventions & Discoveries* (book), 2006

183. Roger Bridgman, *1000 Inventions & Discoveries* (book), 2006

184. 'Submarine Technology through the Years', United States Navy, www.navy.mil, 2000; Dutch Submarines, www.dutchsubmarines.com, 2005

185. 'Tracing the History of the Skyscraper', Suite 101, http://architecture.suite101.com, 2008

186. 'History of Frisbees', Essortment, www.essortment.com, 2002

187. Roger Bridgman, *1000 Inventions & Discoveries* (book), 2006

188. Roger Bridgman, *1000 Inventions & Discoveries* (book), 2006

189. Women Inventors, www.women-inventors.com, 2008

190. Buttery Spreads, www.margarine.org, 2009

191. Kidipede, www.historyforkids.org, 2009; Roger Bridgman, *1000 Inventions & Discoveries* (book), 2006

192. Roger Bridgman, *1000 Inventions & Discoveries* (book), 2006

193. Alternative plastics, www.alternativeplastics.co.uk, 2006; Roger Bridgman, *1000 Inventions & Discoveries* (book), 2006

194. Peugeot, www.peugeot.mainspot.net, 2006

195. Margaret McPhee, *The Dictionary of Australian Inventions and Discoveries* (book), 1993; It's an Honour, www.itsanhonour.gov.au, 2010

196. Broxo, http://eu.broxo.com, 2009; Fein, www.fein.com, 2010

Sources

197. 'History of the Jukebox', Craig Williams Promotions, www.craigwilliams.com.au, 2007

198. Women Inventors, www.women-inventors.com, 2008

199. About.com, http://inventors.about.com, 2010; Trivia-Library.com, www.trivia-library.com, 2004

200. Stephen Van Dulken, *Inventing the 20th Century: 100 Inventions that Shaped the World* (book), 2002

201. Nail Care Salon, www.nailcaresalon.com, 2007; King Tut, www.king-tut.org.uk, 2009

202. Women Inventors, www.women-inventors.com, 2008; Blissymbolics Communication International, www.blissymbolics.org, 2010

203. Women Inventors, www.women-inventors.com, 2008

204. Colin Larkin, *The Encyclopedia of Stage & Film Musicals* (book),1999; Paul Condon and Jim Sangster, *The Complete Hitchcock* (book), 1999

HUMAN BODY

1 Adult skeletons have 206 bones, but babies are born with about 300. You are born with your bones only partly formed, and some of them are invisible on X-ray. As you grow, your bones lengthen and change shape. As you grow up, some bones also fuse together with others to become one. For example, in the thigh, five bones fuse to become the femur. Some bones will keep growing until you are about 25 years old.

 ✓ **FACT**   **OR**   **FICTION**

2 Y̵ou put food into your mouth (ideally a little at a time), chew and then swallow the bits. The stomach produces acid to break up the food into even smaller bits. This stomach acid is strong. Incredibly strong. In fact, it's so strong that your body has to regularly add a new layer to the surface of the stomach. If your body didn't do this, the acid would start to burn holes in the stomach lining, and would eventually burn right through the stomach wall. Ouch!

✓ **FACT**   **OR**   **FICTION**

Freaky Fact or Fiction

3 There are some strange measurement matches related to your body. Measurements that just don't sound right at all. Measure the distance between the crease on the inside of your elbow and the crease inside your wrist. Now measure your foot. If you're flexible enough, double-check and measure your foot against your forearm. It doesn't seem possible, but the length is the same.

✓ FACT OR FICTION

4

Here's another crazy measurement match for you. Have you ever heard people say 'he's as wide as he is tall'? They usually say it about someone who is a little short and round around the tummy. Well, the saying is true for everyone. Stand with your arms stretched out as wide as you can. Have someone measure how wide you are from fingertip to fingertip. Now measure how tall you are. You are as wide as you are tall.

 FACT **OR** **FICTION**

5 Do you ever feel squashed in the back seat of the car? Nothing will ever compare to the squashiness of growing in your mother's tummy. When you are a baby, growing and developing in the womb, you're all folded up, like a contortionist squeezed inside a too-small box. After you're born you start unfolding. And you keep unfolding for the next few years. In many children, the last bit to unfold, or untwist, is the femur, found in the upper leg. It twists outwards so they can walk with their feet pointing forwards.

 ✓ FACT **OR** **FICTION**

6

Many scientists say that humans and apes descended from a common ancestor – and like apes, our ancestor had opposable big toes as well as opposable thumbs. This meant the tip of the big toe could reach and touch the tip of all the other toes, just like you can do with your thumbs. This handy big toe made climbing and balancing easier. As humans evolved, the opposable toe gradually moved. These days all your toes are in line. But the muscles that moved the big toe sideways are still there.

✓ **FACT** **OR** **FICTION**

Freaky Fact or Fiction

Holding a brand-new baby is a tricky thing. They're little and squirmy. Although they have lots of muscles, they haven't learnt how to control them yet. They can't even hold up their head! Their arms and legs move, but they can do very little with them. Human muscle control develops from the head down. First, neck muscles strengthen so the baby can hold up its head and turn it from side-to-side.

Then the baby learns to hold toys, sit up, crawl, stand and walk. Then run!

 ✓ **FACT** **OR** **FICTION**

8 After you die, everything stops. Your heart stops pumping and your blood stops circulating. Your nerves stop sending messages to your brain and back again. Your muscles stop twitching and your body will never need food again. Your skin dries out. But the energy left in your body makes your fingernails and toenails grow, and your hair grows longer, too.

✓ **FACT** **OR** **FICTION**

Freaky Fact or Fiction

What's your favourite food? You can only taste its deliciousness because of tiny cells clustered all over your tongue. These tastebuds are fully developed on your tongue from the instant of your birth. Different tastebuds will detect different tastes. The five recognised groups of tastes are sweet, salty, sour, bitter and umami (savoury). Your body constantly replaces tastebuds, so you will always have more than 10 million on your tongue.

 FACT **OR** **FICTION**

10

Your lungs are under your ribs, above your stomach, below your throat. They take up most of the space in your chest. You have a pair of them: one lung on the right side of your body; one lung on the left. They are the same size and shape and are joined at the trachea (trak-eea), which is also called the windpipe. Each lung has three sections: the superior (upper) lobe, the middle lobe and the inferior (lower) lobe.

✓ **FACT** **OR** **FICTION**

Freaky Fact or Fiction

Your brain is a seething mass of nerve cells. If you were looking at the brain under a very powerful microscope, it would look a bit like a super-full pit of snakes all tangled together. Unlike the snakes, each nerve knows exactly what it is doing and where it's going. Each nerve cell receives information at one end and passes it on at the other, like a giant network of Chinese Whispers or Telephone. Unlike this game, the message remains the same.

✓ **FACT** **OR** **FICTION**

12

The largest part of the brain is the cerebrum, which has two halves (called hemispheres) and sits just beneath the skull. The cerebrum controls your body's movements and stores memories. It's the part of the brain that you see most often in pictures. It's roundish, greyish and full of folds. Have you ever seen a walnut in its shell? Your brain looks just like that. The outer layer of the cerebrum contains 14,000 nerve cells. That's a lot of thinking!

✓ **FACT** **OR** **FICTION**

Freaky Fact or Fiction

Information zooms around the body to and from the brain like a train speeding between stations. Think about how long it takes you to move your hand if it gets too close to something scorching hot. Or how long it takes to lift your foot if you stand on a prickle. Not long. In that time the message has gone from your foot to your brain and back again. At its slowest, the message moves at about 3.6 km/h (2.25 mi/h). At its fastest, the message zooms along at around 108 km/h (67.5 mi/h), about the same speed as a car on a freeway.

✓ FACT OR FICTION

14 An Adam's apple is called that because it looks like a small apple that has stuck in your throat. The Adam's apple is part of your larynx, also known as your voice box. If you are a boy, your Adam's apple will appear at the front of your neck during puberty, when every part of your body seems to be growing.

The cartilage of the Adam's apple also grows in girls during puberty, but is usually smaller and less obvious.

 FACT **OR** **FICTION**

15

There are two tubes in your throat. One, the trachea (trak-eea), is for breathing and leads to your lungs. The other, the oesophagus (ee-sof-a-gus), is for food and leads to your stomach. It's not often that the wrong stuff goes into the wrong tube. Why? Because the food tube has a lid called the epiglottis (eppy-gloh-tus). It's a bit like a flip-top bin. The epiglottis closes over the food tube every time you swallow.

✓ FACT   OR   FICTION

16 ave you ever wondered what the fuss is about with Brussels sprouts? Why lots of kids hate them but some older people like them as much as chocolate? It's to do (partly) with tastebuds. Kids just have more – tastebuds that is. Each tastebud lives for about a week, then is replaced with a new one. In adults, some of the tastebuds are not replaced as quickly and sometimes not at all. So, older people have fewer tastebuds. Perhaps that explains Brussels sprouts. Or not.

 ✓ **FACT** **OR** **FICTION**

Freaky Fact or Fiction

A real smile (rather than a pretend I'm-not-really-happy-but-I-know-you-want-me-to smile type) doesn't just involve your mouth but the whole of your face. Your mouth stretches, your cheeks are raised and you get little wrinkles (or crow's feet) in the corners of your eyes. If you want to be sure that someone is REALLY smiling, check to see if these other parts of their face move. If not, perhaps their heart isn't in it.

✓ FACT OR FICTION

18

Your brain grows faster than your face. Your brain and skull are almost completely grown by the time you are six years old. When you are born, four-fifths of your head is brain and skull and only one-fifth of your head is face. By the time you reach adulthood, your face is about half the size of your head.

✓ **FACT** **OR** **FICTION**

19

When you were a baby, you breathed faster than you do now, and much faster than you will when you are an adult. You breathed about 33 times a minute when you were a baby. By the time you are an adult your breathing will have slowed to less than half that rate. An adult breathes about 14 times a minute. For each baby-breathing minute, you breathed in about 500 mL (about 1 pt) of air. As an adult you will breathe in about 7 L (14 pt) every minute.

✓ FACT OR FICTION

20

Babies are born without bony kneecaps. The kneecap is a special kind of bone called a sesamoid. It should be called the secret bone. Sesamoid bones form inside tendons that move over bony surfaces (like when your knee bends). The kneecap, or patella, develops inside the tendon at the front of your knee from when you are about two years old. It helps to make sure you can run and jump and skip without getting all wobbly.

 ✓ FACT   OR   FICTION

21

Y ou have between 200,000 and 500,000 sweat glands on your skin. That means an average of between 15 and 34 per square centimetre (about 6 to 14 per square inch) of your skin. There are more on the palms of your hands and soles of your feet than other parts of your body. Mostly, sweat glands are there to cool your skin, but those on the palms and soles are designed to keep the skin moist and soft so you can hang on tight.

 FACT **OR** **FICTION**

22

There are about 150,000 hair follicles on the head. Each hair goes through three phases in its life. The first is an active growing phase, when the hair gets longer and longer. This phase can last for several years. The second is a resting phase, when the hair no longer grows. Perhaps it needs a snooze after all that growing. After the resting phase is finished, a new hair begins to grow, pushing out the old one. This is the third phase: shedding. Every day you shed about 50 to 100 hairs.

 ✓ **FACT** **OR** **FICTION**

23 A cough is a good thing. Really. A cough is a rapid explosion of air out of your lungs. Your body uses a cough reflex to make sure nothing but air gets into your lungs. If you accidentally breathe in something else, like dust, or a fly, or the mucus that comes with a cold, you will cough to push it straight back out again. Coughs have been measured at over 100 km/h (60 mi/h).

 FACT **OR** **FICTION**

24

Most muscles in the body have a single job. For example, one muscle's job is to bend the elbow. Another muscle will straighten it. But the tongue is a special collection of muscle cells with many jobs to do. It moves food around the mouth while you are chewing. It ensures saliva is mixed with the food bits to make them moist. When chewing is finished, the tongue pushes the food to the back of your throat and into your oesophagus (ee-sof-a-gus) for swallowing. The tongue also helps you to talk.

 FACT **OR** **FICTION**

25

The outer ear, the part you can see and feel, is called the auricle. Around the auricle are several small muscles that attach it to the skull and scalp. These muscles are similar in all animals with outer ears. If you try hard, you can move your ears up and down and away from your head, just like a dog or a cat can.

✓ **FACT** **OR** **FICTION**

26

Your ears and nose will continue to grow all your life. When you are born, your ears and nose are quite tiny. As the rest of you grows, they grow along with you. But most of you stops growing when you reach adulthood. Not your ears, or your nose. They will keep growing until the day you die.

 ✓ **FACT**   **OR**   **FICTION**

Freaky Fact or Fiction

You may be familiar with the names for many parts of your body. A foot is a foot. A nose is a nose. But there are names for parts of the body that you may not know as well. The name for the space between your eyebrows is called the glabella (glah-bell-a) and the name for your nasal passage is called the meatus (mee-ar-tus or mee-ate-us).

✓ **FACT** **OR** **FICTION**

28

ook at your baby photos. Look at your fingers, your toes, your nose. Most bits of you are tiny, tiny, tiny. Your body has lots of growing to do after you are born. But not your eyes. Your eyes are almost as big as they will ever be. Newborn babies' eyes are over 2/3 of the size that they will become in adulthood, so they really don't grow much more at all.

✓ **FACT** **OR** **FICTION**

29

There are 22 bones in your head. Eight form part of your cranium (the bit covered by hair) and 14 are part of your face. Together, the 22 bones are known as your skull. When you are born your cranium bones aren't completely formed and there are six soft spots on your head called fontanelles. The largest of these is on top of your head, towards the front. These soft spots disappear as your cranium bones join together and harden. They usually have all disappeared by the time you are three months old.

✓ **FACT** **OR** **FICTION**

30

Imagine if you grew fingernails on your head, or if hair sprouted from your fingertips. It would be so uncomfortable to sleep and hair would always be getting in your food. Luckily, it doesn't work that way. But fingernails, toenails and hair are made from the same cells, just arranged differently. Your fingernails grow twice as fast as your toenails do, and slower than your hair. Fingernails take about three months to grow from the skin fold at the base to the free edge. Toenails take about twice that time. Hair grows about three times faster than your fingernails.

✓ **FACT** **OR** **FICTION**

Freaky Fact or Fiction

31 Not all hair is the same. Not even on your body. Imagine if all the hairs on your body grew to the same length as your head hair. Hairdressers would love it! They'd be busy seven days a week, trimming your arm hairs and your leg hairs, as well as the hair on your head. And everyone, male and female, would have hair all over their face, even on their forehead. Your eyelashes would cover your eyes! But luckily, the body is cleverer than that. Eyelashes only grow long enough to keep dust out of your eyes.

 ✓ **FACT**   **OR**   **FICTION**

32

ook closely at a hair from your head. Compare it with a friend's hair. The colour might be different and you may be able to see a difference in thickness, but mostly it looks the same. Look under a microscope and you can see that they're not the same at all. If you cut across a hair, and look end-on, straight hair is flat. Wavy hair is round in some parts, oval in others. And very curly hair looks almost perfectly round.

✓ **FACT** **OR** **FICTION**

33

It's never a lot of fun to have a cold. But just for a minute, think about the tiny virus that causes the cold. Your body's first response to the virus is to create more and more mucus in your nose to try to flood out the virus. When that doesn't work, the irritation in the nose causes you to sneeze to try to explode the pesky thing out. Then you start coughing to eject the virus from your lungs. How unwanted must the virus feel?

 ✓ **FACT**   **OR**   **FICTION**

34

Vomiting is the forcible ejection of the stomach contents via your mouth. It is never much fun. Usually you feel rotten beforehand and sometimes, even afterwards. The feeling starts deep in your stomach and moves upwards until there's nowhere to go but out. Along the way, muscles squeeze, one after another to keep the vomit moving along, just like squeezing the stuffing out of a raw sausage. But faster.

✓ **FACT** **OR** **FICTION**

Freaky Fact or Fiction

35

How is growing a beard like joining the dots? Both start with an outline and join up later. In puberty, boys begin to grow new hair all over their bodies, including on their faces. Facial hair appears in a particular order. The first bits appear above the corners of the mouth, then gradually above the top lip. Next the cheeks, then under the middle of the lower lip. Finally all the bits join up. Voila! A beard.

✓ **FACT** **OR** **FICTION**

36

Do you always eat everything on your plate? Even if you do, not everything you eat can be used by your body. The food moves through your stomach, small intestine and then your large intestine. In your large intestine (or bowel), bacteria helps to break down the last bit of usable food. Each day when you open your bowels (do number twos, or poo) you release more than three teaspoons full of bacteria.

✓ **FACT** **OR** **FICTION**

37

Gurgle, gurgle, burble. Listen to your own belly, or to the belly of someone else. (It's easier to get close to someone else's belly!) That gurgling noise has a special name: borborygmi (bor-boh-rig-mee). It's gas moving through the intestine. It's part nitrogen, part oxygen, part hydrogen, part methane and part carbon dioxide. What a mix! Guess what the gas is called when it makes it all the way through the intestines and leaves your body? That's right – flatus (flay-tuss)!

 ✓ **FACT**   **OR**   **FICTION**

38 Milk contains lactose, which is milk sugar. Not everyone can digest lactose. Those who can't break down lactose into usable bits suffer from lactose intolerance. If a lactose-intolerant person drinks a glass of milk, the milk travels all the way through to the large intestine without being digested. There it mixes with bacteria and makes gas. Lots of it. One cup of hydrogen gas for each glass of milk! Oh, poor stretched tummy. Only one way out for that gas.

 FACT OR **FICTION**

39

The small intestine is like a rubbery, slippery, twisty tube a bit fatter than a garden hose. It connects the stomach with the large intestine. If it were stretched out in one straight line, it would measure about 7 m (23 ft). But it's not stretched out. It's curled up inside your belly like one long loopy piece of spaghetti. That's longer than a skipping rope and about the same as 23 bits of spaghetti laid end to end.

✓ FACT OR FICTION

40

Do you get tired walking to school? Or walking home? Just remember to count the steps. If you work out how far each step is, you can work out how many kilometres (miles) you walk each day. If you add up the footsteps of a lifetime and convert them into kilometres (miles), you can work out how far you will walk in a lifetime. The average person will walk more than three times around the world. That's about 128,000 km (80,000 mi). Hope you're wearing comfortable shoes!

 ✓ **FACT**   **OR**   **FICTION**

Freaky Fact or Fiction

41

Some people say that you can predict how tall someone will be by doubling the height they are at two years old. But one man in Austria, Adam Rainer (1899–1950), grew at his own rate. At 21 years old, Adam was only 1.18 m (3 ft 10.5 in) tall. Then he had a growth spurt. Over the next 10 years, he almost doubled his height, reaching 2.18 m (7 ft 1.75 in). If the prediction was true for him, Adam would have been about the same height at two years old that he was on his 21st birthday.

✓ **FACT**   **OR**   **FICTION**

42

A tongue is a handy thing. It's great for licking an ice-cream, swallowing and talking. Not all tongues are the same. Just as there are tall people and tiny people, tongues are different sizes. The longest tongue ever measured was 9.8 cm (3.9 in) from the tip to the centre of the top lip. The tongue's owner was Stephen Taylor from the United Kingdom, who stuck his tongue out for posterity in February 2009. That's one man you wouldn't want to share your ice-cream with – he'd have it all in just one lick.

✓ **FACT** **OR** **FICTION**

43

How did you learn to count? Did you use your fingers and toes? Everyone has 10 fingers and 10 toes, right? Not quite. Most people do, but a few people have more, and a few have less. People with polydactyly (poll-ee-dac-til-ee) have more. The most digits ever recorded on a living person is 25. This record is shared by Pranamya Menaria (born 10 August 2005) and Devendra Harne (born 9 January 1995), both from India. The Wadoma and Kalanga tribes of Africa could use some of the extras. Some of them are born with only two toes on each foot.

 ✓ **FACT**   **OR** **FICTION**

44

Have you got a very loud brother or sister? Or are you the loud one in the family? It's hard to be quiet all the time, especially when you have friends over to play, or for dinner. But who do you think could make the loudest burp? Male or female? You'd be surprised. It was a woman! The loudest burp ever recorded was very loud – nearly 105 decibels. That's almost as loud as a jackhammer or a power saw.

 FACT **OR** **FICTION**

Freaky Fact or Fiction

45

Sharks keep growing new teeth all their lives but it doesn't work that way for humans. Baby teeth grow and fall out and permanent teeth arrive. Except for wisdom teeth, most of your permanent teeth will have arrived by the time you're a teenager. Then that's it. Once you're an adult, you're finished with growing teeth. Look after them because they're the only teeth you'll ever get. Single teeth can appear later, but it's rare. It happened to Mária Pozderka of Hungary (born 19 July 1938) – she got a new tooth when she was 68 years old.

 FACT **OR** **FICTION**

46

Imagine someone said to you, 'Here – you can have one handful of chocolates.' That's one of the times it would be great to have the biggest hands in the world. The biggest hands in the world belonged to American Robert Wadlow (1918–1940) and measured 32.4 cm (12.75 in) from the wrist to the tip of the middle finger. Even better would be if someone said you could have one shoeful of chocolates and you had the biggest feet in the world. Robert's feet measured 47 cm (18.5 in) in length.

 ✓ FACT   **OR**   **FICTION**

47

I scream, you scream, we all scream for ice-cream! Anyone serving you, me or us at the ice-cream counter might want to wear earphones. Or they might send us away without anything. Or tell us to ask again, but quietly. There's nothing gentle or quiet about a scream. The loudest scream recorded was by Jill Drake (UK) in 2000. At 129 dB, her scream was almost as loud as a shotgun firing, or a jet plane taking off. Ouch!

 FACT **OR** **FICTION**

48

Have you ever wanted to grow your hair? Cut out all that wasted time sitting in the hairdresser's chair? You'd better get started if you're hoping to set a new world record. The record for the longest hair is currently held by Xie Qiuping, a Chinese woman who has been growing her locks since she was 13 years old. When it was last measured in 2004 she was 44 years old and her hair was 5.627 m (18 ft 5.54 in) long.

 FACT **OR** **FICTION**

Freaky Fact or Fiction

There's nothing more irritating than an itch you just can't reach. Like an itch in the middle of your back. You can almost reach it over your shoulder but just not quite. Longer arms might help. Or longer fingernails. But you always have to cut your fingernails to keep them clean and tidy. Lee Redmond, a woman in the US, could scratch any itch she liked. In 2008, her fingernails were measured at a combined length of 8.65 m (28 ft 4.5 in). On average, that means each fingernail was around 86.5 cm (2 ft 10 in).

✓ **FACT** **OR** **FICTION**

Human Body

50

The human body needs to be cleaned from time to time, and there's nothing like a hot, steaming bath at the end of a long, dirty day. Especially if it is a big bath and includes lots of bubbles. Perfect for a long soak. But there are some baths you might think twice (or more) about before hopping in. There are those who think a bath of ice is wonderful, and there are legends about baths in milk. But the worst bath would have to be the one shared with 87 snakes. Hard to imagine that being fun at all.

✓ **FACT** **OR** **FICTION**

51

Seven litres of water would more than half-fill a bucket. It's more than enough to wash the breakfast dishes. It would fill a glass about 30 times, or 30 glasses once. It is enough water to handwash a car, and more than enough to quench a thirst. It's also the amount of digestive fluid released into the human digestive tract every day.

 ✓ FACT OR FICTION

52

If you peeled off your skin, you'd be able to see all the muscles that help your body to move, but you don't need to do anything quite that drastic. By moving your limbs you can easily feel many of the bigger muscles. But there are other little muscles that are harder to feel. In total, there are about 100 muscles that help humans to do all the amazing things they can do. Together they make up about 30 per cent of your body weight.

✓ **FACT** **OR** **FICTION**

Freaky Fact or Fiction

53

Breathe in. Breathe out. When you breathe in, you open out all the tiny sacs in your lungs and fill them with air. Together these air sacs look a little like bunches of grapes all linked by tiny stems. When you breathe out, the sacs all sag. If you were to open out all the tiny sacs and place them side-by-side on a flat surface, they would cover almost 140 m² (1500 ft²). That's about the size of a classroom.

✓ **FACT** OR **FICTION**

54

Kidneys are the same shape as a kidney bean. About the same colour too, but bigger. Kidneys generally come in pairs, one sitting either side of your body close to your back. They are about 10 cm (4 in) long and filter (clean) all your blood (about 5 L or 1.3 gal) every 45 minutes. That adds up to more than 160 L (over 35 gal) of blood filtered each day. All that's left after the clean blood returns to the blood vessels is about 1.4 L (3 pt) of liquid that the body gets rid of as urine (wee or pee).

✓ **FACT** **OR** **FICTION**

Freaky Fact or Fiction

Does your body always do what you tell it to? Do you sometimes miss when you're trying to hit a cricket ball or tennis ball? Sometimes it seems like someone else is in charge. Your body has different types of muscles. Some are called 'voluntary' muscles, which means you can move them where you want. Other muscles, like the ones that keep your heart beating, and the ones that push your food through your stomach and intestine, are called 'involuntary'. They keep on working when you are awake or asleep. They keep on working even when you hit or miss that ball.

 FACT OR FICTION

56

In movies sometimes blood is shown spurting from a wound, bright and pulsing. This will only happen if the bleeding is from an artery, because only arteries are made with tiny muscles. Muscles squeeze the blood through the arteries and around the body and can be felt as a pulse. Veins have no muscles at all. If a vein is cut, the blood trickles out.

 ✓ **FACT** **OR** **FICTION**

Freaky Fact or Fiction

57

Doctors and nurses look for pulses as a way to see how the heart is going (or IF it is still going). All arteries will pulse, but they're not all easy to find. It's a bit tricky to find your own pulse because the fingers you use to feel for it will have their own faint pulse. Common places to feel the pulse are inside the wrist, at the side-front of the neck, at the temple and behind the knee.

 FACT   **OR**   **FICTION**

58

Blood is red, right? Right. What about the blue veins that you can see through your skin? It isn't really blue. Blood in the veins is a dark red colour. It just shows blue through your pink skin. Blood in arteries is bright red. It's the amount of oxygen in the blood that changes the colour. The more oxygen, the brighter red the blood.

✓ **FACT** **OR** **FICTION**

Freaky Fact or Fiction

59 Lurking deep in your bloodstream are white blood cells called 'natural killers' or NK cells. Some white blood cells exist to kill any invaders such as viruses or infections – cells that don't belong in your blood. But natural killers are different. Their role is to turn on your body's own cells, then kill them. But don't worry, they only kill your own cells if the cells are damaged or diseased.

 FACT **OR** **FICTION**

60

There's nothing worse than having bugs crawling on your skin. Oh, yes there is! It's much worse having bugs crawling inside your body, making you sick. In the disease called schistosomiasis (shiss-to-so-my-uh-sis), a tiny flatworm squirms through your skin and lays between 30 and 50 eggs per day into the bloodstream. Your body evicts the eggs when you go to the toilet. Yay! The eggs hatch and grow (in snails) and then when they are big enough, the new flatworms can burrow back into your body to feed. Not so yay!

 FACT **OR** **FICTION**

Freaky Fact or Fiction

What do humans and sheep have in common? Not their coats – sheep win there. Not their feet – sheep have twice as many feet and no hands. Not their conversation – sheep don't have a lot to say. Horns? Surprisingly that's what they have in common with humans. If you permanently damage a fingernail or a toenail, it will grow thick, ridgy and curved – just like a ram's horns do. In fact, toenails and fingernails that grow like that are called 'ram's horn nails'.

 FACT **OR** **FICTION**

If you thought hives were just for bees, think again. Hives are a very, very itchy, lumpy, reddish, whitish skin reaction to something. There's no honey in these hives! Sometimes the reaction is to a food, like peanuts or shellfish. But another form of hives is dermatographism (der-mat-o-graf-ism), or skin writing. When you 'write' on the sufferer's skin by touching it or stroking it with an object, the skin reacts by swelling and becoming red. You can then actually read their skin. It's a bit like a temporary tattoo.

✓ **FACT** **OR** **FICTION**

Freaky Fact or Fiction

Are you scared of spiders? Snakes? Going outside your home? When a fear begins to affect the way you live your life, it's called a phobia. Most phobias have names. There are well-known phobias like arachnophobia (fear of spiders) and claustrophobia (fear of enclosed spaces). But there are many others. How about tremophobia? That's a fear of trembling. People with limnophobia are scared of lakes. There's even a name for people who are scared of developing a phobia. They have phobophobia!

 ✓ **FACT** **OR** **FICTION**

64

Puberty (when your body begins to change from a child to an adult) is a bit like spring. Very difficult to predict and to measure. Hormone levels go up and down like the temperature. Hair appears like new leaves. All sorts of other bits grow like crazy. Parents complain about having to keep buying new shoes. Not everything keeps up though. Usually when you stand up, your body adjusts your blood flow so you don't get light-headed or dizzy. But if you grow taller too fast, sometimes if you stand up suddenly, you might feel a little dizzy, or you might faint.

✓ **FACT** **OR** **FICTION**

65

Plant some seeds in good soil, water them and they will grow. Hang on – there's one more thing you need. Sunlight. Without sunlight, or with not enough sunlight, plants will not grow strong, if at all. Luckily you are not a plant. As long as you have enough good food, water and exercise, you will grow strong and healthy.

✓ **FACT** **OR** **FICTION**

66

ailing, even just for a few hours, can make you very hungry. It's all that fresh air and work moving the sails to the right position. But it's usually just for fun and you're never very far from shore. Or food. It was much more difficult for long-distance sailors in the days before there were fridges. They might have been at sea for months, and fresh fruit and vegetables were the first foods to run out. Some sailors developed scurvy from the lack of Vitamin C. They became very grumpy, their teeth fell out and they had no energy for anything.

 ✓ FACT **OR** **FICTION**

67

Don't cry. It makes your eyes all red and puffy and your face all blotchy. Amazing, you might think, since tears are simply salty water. Actually they're not. Well, not completely. There is salty water in tears. Tears also include oil, which helps to stop the water evaporating, and mucus, which helps the water to spread evenly across your eyeball.

 ✓ FACT **OR** **FICTION**

68

Make your fortune! Bring out the oil drills! Your body is covered in tiny oil wells. There are even oil glands along your eyelids. These tiny oil glands help to keep the eye moist. They are on the upper and lower eyelids and there can be between 50 and 70 in each eye. So many oil glands, but so tiny. Perhaps put away those oil drills. Not enough oil here to make any money.

✓ **FACT** **OR** **FICTION**

69

Long words, short words. The weight or importance of a word is not measured by its length. It's the same with the body. A hip is a hip whether you call it so or use its proper name, *articulatio coxae*. Here are eight more body words that have just three letters. Big and small, we need them all. Eye, leg, arm, toe, jaw, rib, lip and gum.

 ✓ FACT **OR** **FICTION**

70

'Blink and you'll miss it' is a common expression. It usually means that something is very fast. Like a train, or a bird. Luckily most things move slower than that so you can see them. Just as well. The average person blinks about 12 times every minute, usually once every two to 10 seconds. That's 720 times an hour, 17,280 times per day and around 6,307,200 times per year. Imagine what you could miss!

✓ **FACT** **OR** **FICTION**

71

Have you ever had a craving for eating clay, paper or other weird non-food things? It's different to when babies just put everything in their mouth. It's a medical condition where people want to eat things that are not food. It's called 'pica' (peek-ah). Doctors are not sure what causes it, but sometimes it happens in people with anaemia (with a lack of red blood cells, or red blood cells not working properly). Sufferers sometimes crave ice and say it tastes better than it does when they're well.

 FACT **OR** **FICTION**

72

ave a close look at your face in the mirror. Look at the faces of your family and friends. Any freckles there? Look at a baby or small child. Check your parents. Freckles don't usually appear in children under two years old. They tend to disappear in adults too. But even someone who has many, many freckles on their face won't have freckles on the parts of their skin that have not been out in the sun. (Like in their armpit, or on their bottom!)

 FACT **OR** **FICTION**

Freaky Fact or Fiction

73

Have you ever wondered why your nose gets runny when you cry? It's bad enough that your eyes overflow. Why does your nose have to do the same? Perhaps your nose just wants to be part of the action. When you cry, your nose begins to produce more mucus (snot or boogers). This mucus collects and then runs out of your nose, just like the tears run down your cheeks.

 FACT **OR** **FICTION**

74

Lub-dub. Lub-dub. That's the sound of your heart beating. If you ever get a chance to listen through a stethoscope, that's the sound you'll hear. It's the sound of the heart working to pump blood around the body. From when you are born until you are an adult, your heartbeat gradually slows down until, on average, it happens about 70 times a minute. That's 4200 times an hour, 100,800 times a day and nearly 37 million times in a year.

✓ **FACT** **OR** **FICTION**

Freaky Fact or Fiction

75

An adult human heart beats around 70 times per minute. In general, the smaller an animal is, the slower its heart rate will be. The larger an animal the faster its heart rate will be. A canary has a heart rate of about 25 beats per minute. An elephant's heart rate is about 1000 beats per minute.

✓ FACT OR FICTION

76

Do you sometimes feel invisible? People with Cotard's syndrome do. Sometimes they think they have no heart, or no stomach. Sometimes it's so bad that even though they know they are walking around, they are sure they're dead. They continue to believe this, even when they are reassured that they are alive. Sometimes they are also convinced that the world doesn't exist anymore. Not a happy place.

✓ **FACT** **OR** **FICTION**

77

Health experts suggest that eating fish is a good thing to do. It's lower in fat than beef and pork and has other healthy benefits. And it's delicious. But even if you love the taste of fish, you probably would rather not smell like one. Particularly one that's died at sea and washed up onto the beach and is super-rotten and pongy. People with 'fish odour syndrome' smell like those fish. They have fishy breath and their sweat also smells like rotting fish.

 FACT   **OR**   **FICTION**

78

The first successful kidney transplant was performed by a medical team in Boston, USA, in 1954. The first successful heart transplant was performed by South African surgeon Christiaan Barnard in 1967. Since then medical science has discovered how to successfully transplant many different organs, including liver, bone marrow, cornea, lungs and more. Maybe one day they will be able to transplant every part of your body. Imagine!

✓ FACT OR FICTION

79

ometimes when people are very cold, their lips and fingers can appear blue. But the blue soon disappears when the person warms up again. Their skin colour returns to a normal pinky colour. The blue colour is not permanent. Unless of course you have argyria (ar-jir-ee-a). People with this condition have blue skin. Their gums, fingernails and toenails can also be blue. And it's nothing to do with the cold. It's caused by a build-up of silver inside their body.

 ✓ FACT **OR** **FICTION**

80

Where on your body would you find a philtrum? What do you do with a philtrum? How many of them are there? Well, there's only one and it's on your face. It's the vertical groove above your upper lip, just below the middle of your nose. It's where some men grow a tiny moustache. And it doesn't really do very much at all. It just is.

✓ FACT   OR   FICTION

Freaky Fact or Fiction

81

Would you like to be taller? Almost instantly? Then head out of your house, out of your town, out of this world. The place you want is space. In space, you weigh nothing, and you become taller. All you have to do is finish school and university, join a space program and take off. Easy! In space, or anywhere else where there is no gravity, you could soon be about 3 per cent taller.

 FACT **OR** **FICTION**

82

Is it a bird? Is it a crocodile? Is it a dolphin? Is it human? Surely you can tell the difference! They're nothing alike. Perhaps not now, but if you look at the bones of these animals' forearms you may see some similarities. Many scientists believe they all evolved from a common ancestor. They may be different sizes and the proportions different, but the same bones are there. It's lucky we don't have to assemble our bodies from a kit. Imagine if you picked the wrong bits and ended up with short stumpy crocodile forelegs instead of forearms.

 FACT **OR** **FICTION**

Freaky Fact or Fiction

83

Imagine having a sibling that is with you for your entire life. Everywhere you go, they go too. Whenever they speak, you can hear them. That is what conjoined twins experience. Conjoined twins are identical twins who are physically joined when they are born. The most well-known conjoined twins are Eng and Chang Bunker, who were born in Siam (now Thailand) in 1811. They were joined at the lower chest, but other conjoined twins have been born joined at the hip, the stomach and even the head! Thanks to developments in surgery, it is now possible for some (but not all) conjoined twins to be separated.

 FACT   **OR**   **FICTION**

84

Dust is just a bit of dirt, isn't it? Well, there may be soil in dust but there are also many other ingredients. House dust includes wool, cotton, paper fibres, fingernail clippings, food crumbs, pollen, foam particles, salt and sugar crystals, animal dander (dog and cat skin and fur), fungal spores and wood shavings! It also includes quite a lot of human skin flakes. Every day, breathing in all that stuff – it's almost enough to make you WANT to clean your bedroom. Almost.

✓ **FACT** **OR** **FICTION**

Freaky Fact or Fiction

85

Dust mites are related to spiders and have eight legs. They are so tiny you can hardly see them, but they are there in their thousands. Their favourite food is flaked-off skin. Yum. Yum. They crawl around your bed and pillow. Delightful. Some people are allergic to dust mites, but for most people, dust mites don't cause any problems as long as you change your sheets regularly and vacuum every once in a while.

 ✓ **FACT**   **OR**   **FICTION**

86 ave you ever had a blister? Perhaps on your hand from swinging on the monkey bars, or on your foot where a shoe has rubbed. It's usually no big deal and though it might hurt for a little while, it soon heals and is forgotten. But there is a rare condition called epidermolysis bullosa (epp-ee-derm-o-ly-sis bull-o-sa) where blisters can never be forgotten. People with epidermolysis bullosa have very fragile skin and their blisters can be enormous and leave scars.

✓ **FACT** **OR** **FICTION**

Freaky Fact or Fiction

87

Do you bite your nails? It's not the most attractive of habits. Think of all the germs that you swallow with the bits of nails. Even if you spit out the nails, some of the germs stay in your mouth. Like all habits, it's a hard one to break. It even has its own medical name. It's called onychophagia (on-ick-o-fay-jah). The word literally means finger-mouth.

 ✓ **FACT** **OR** **FICTION**

88

Melanin gives colour to your skin. Being in the sun causes your body to produce more melanin, to help protect you from the sun. But some people, those with albinism, have less or no melanin in their skin, hair and eyes. Animals with albinism will lack melanin in their feathers or scales. They will look white. People with albinism often have very pale skin and hair. But they do have good night-sight.

✓ FACT OR FICTION

89

Some things are good and some things are bad. Ice-cream is good? Yes. Bacteria is bad? Well, yes and no. There are good and bad bacteria and your intestines are full of the good kind (if you are healthy). Your body needs the good bacteria to help break down food into bits that the body can use. In fact, an average adult carries about 1.5 kg (3.3 lb) of good bacteria in their intestines. Bad bacteria are the ones that make you sick. Just as well your body can tell the difference.

 FACT **OR** **FICTION**

90

Have you ever heard people talking about someone wearing 'rose-coloured glasses'? Usually it means that they are being too optimistic, or not realistic about something or someone. If you have cyanopsia (sy-an-op-see-a), however, you see everything with a blueish tinge. And if you have acyanopsia, you can't recognise blue at all.

 FACT **OR** **FICTION**

Freaky Fact or Fiction

91 Achromatopsia (ay-crow-ma-top-see-a) is total colour-blindness and is very rare. More common is colour-blindness to just one colour. If you had red colour-blindness you'd find it hard to tell the difference between red and green. If you were blue-blind, you'd struggle to tell the difference between blue and yellow. And if you were green-blind, you just wouldn't be able to see green.

✓ **FACT** **OR** **FICTION**

92 About one in every 10 boys and girls has colour-blindness. That means there could be more than one colour-blind child in every classroom. Children with red-green colour-blindness have trouble telling the difference between red and green. The condition can be hereditary, programmed in your genes before you are born. If both your parents carry a gene for colour-blindness there's a chance you will have it too.

✓ **FACT** **OR** **FICTION**

93

The biggest artery in the body is the aorta (ay-ort-ah). It is about 3 cm (about 1 in) in diameter. Make a circle with your thumb and first finger. It's about that big. The smallest blood vessels are the capillaries (cap-ill-ah-rees), which are only about one cell wide. If you put all the blood vessels together, end to end, they would reach twice around the world.

 FACT OR **FICTION**

94

The heart is very hardworking. Each minute it pumps 5 L (about 10.6 pt) of blood around the body. That's the total volume of blood for an average adult. So, that's 5 L a minute, 300 L an hour, 7200 L a day. That's more than 2.5 million L (660,000 gal) of blood pumped through the heart in one single year. That's about the volume of water in an Olympic-sized pool. That's a lot of pumping. Especially for a pump that is only the size of your clenched fist.

✓ FACT OR FICTION

Freaky Fact or Fiction

95 Humans and sharks – they're very different creatures. Instead of legs, sharks have fins. Sharks have tails; humans don't. Sharks live in water; humans live on land. Sharks have gills; humans have lungs. But there is one way, at least, where sharks and humans are similar. The cornea of the shark eye is very similar to the human cornea. In fact, it is so similar that shark corneas have been transplanted into humans. Corneas help humans (and sharks) to see.

✓ FACT   OR FICTION

96

ACHHHOOOOO! You closed your eyes! ACHOO! ACHOO! You closed them again. Next time you sneeze, see if you can keep your eyes open. It's almost impossible. That's because a sneeze is a reflex that affects more than just your nose. Your face muscles, throat and chest are also involved. First something irritates your nose. Then you take in a big breath ... a ... ahh. Then you breathe out very quickly and violently to clear your nose. ACHOO!

 FACT **OR** **FICTION**

Freaky Fact or Fiction

When you sneeze, air and other bits (hopefully including whatever caused the sneeze) are exploded from your nose. Fast. Faster than you can run. Faster than a speeding bicycle. Faster than a cheetah sprinting. The speed of a sneeze can be up to 150 km/h (about 93 mi/h). If your sneeze was a cyclone, it would be classed as a Category 1: gale. Damage to crops and trees. Might drag boats from their moorings.

✓ FACT   OR   FICTION

98

Have you ever sleepwalked? Chances are you don't remember it. Sleepwalkers seldom do. But they can sit up and climb out of bed. Sleepwalkers sometimes get dressed. They may walk with their eyes open and can find their way around corners. You can even have a conversation with a sleepwalker, although they may not make all that much sense. Amazing. And they have no memory of any of this the next day.

 ✓ **FACT** **OR** **FICTION**

99

Frog. Snake. Human. That's how your heart develops. Huh? When you were growing in the womb, your heart started out as just a collection of cells, then a tube. For a while it looked like a frog's heart, with only two chambers. Next it developed a third chamber and began to look more like a snake's heart. Final stop was four chambers and then your heart looked just like it should. Four chambers, all contributing to pumping your blood to your head, to your fingers and your toes.

 ✓ FACT OR FICTION

100

It seems that everything in the body has a name. Even the mashed-up food that leaves your stomach on the way to the small intestine has a name. It's called chyme (kyme). Chyme is a thick liquid that sits in your stomach for hours. Then it is spurted into your intestine in little bursts. That soupy mush used to be your favourite food. It doesn't look so yum now!

✓ **FACT** **OR** **FICTION**

Freaky Fact or Fiction

101

Sphincters (sfink-ters) are like rubber bands. They are ring-like muscles that tighten and close around different tubes in your body. They tighten to close and relax to open. There are sphincters at the top and bottom of your stomach – a bit like having ties at each end of a balloon. There are also sphincters around the bottom of the large bowel and at the end of the urethra. Lucky really, because if there were no sphincters at these two places, you'd have to wear a nappy for your entire life!

✓ **FACT** **OR** **FICTION**

102

Sphincters (sfink-ters) are ring-like muscles that open and close to control what goes in and what comes out of certain sections of your body. One sphincter you can easily see is your iris. If someone shines a bright light into your eye, the sphincter shrinks or tightens. If you are trying to read in bed after lights out, your iris will relax and let in as much light as possible.

✓ **FACT** **OR** **FICTION**

Freaky Fact or Fiction

Yawn. There's nothing nicer than crawling into bed at the end of a long, busy day and sleeping. First you close your eyes, then relax your body and gradually, gently, your body drifts off to dreamland. It doesn't work like that for people who experience narcolepsy (nark-o-lep-see). They can fall asleep very suddenly. For example, you might be in the middle of telling them the most exciting story and they will fall asleep. On their feet. Then, a few minutes later, they'll wake up just as suddenly, and can tell you exactly what you were saying while they were asleep.

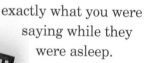

 FACT   **OR**   **FICTION**

104 It's hard to get moving some mornings. You just want to turn over and slip back into that dream about being on a beach in the sun. But you can't. You have to get up to go to school and eventually that's just what you do. But if you have narcolepsy (nark-o-lep-see) you can't always do that. Get up, that is. Some people with narcolepsy wake up in the morning but can't move anything. They are paralysed, although their brain is awake. Scary. Luckily it doesn't usually last for long and they too can get up and get ready for school!

✓ **FACT**   **OR**   **FICTION**

Freaky Fact or Fiction

Laughing is great fun. From the tiniest chuckle to the biggest, shake-the-walls guffaw, laughing helps you to feel better. But have you ever laughed so much you couldn't stand up? Have you ever fallen over laughing? People who do may have dogaplexy, a condition where you briefly lose control of your muscles and fall over.

✓ FACT   OR   FICTION

106

Has anyone ever told you to go to bed because you are tired and grumpy? When you are extremely tired, it's hard to make sense of anything. It can seem too hard to brush your teeth or even to put on your pyjamas. Extreme tiredness from lack of sleep is called sleep deprivation (deh-pri-vay-shun). Some other symptoms of sleep deprivation include blurry eyes, hard-to-understand speech and being confused. Nighty-night. Off to bed with you!

✓ **FACT** **OR** **FICTION**

107

Ouch! Sometimes when you fall over or fall out of a tree, or fall out of a tree and then fall over, you scrape skin. Sometimes it feels like you've taken off many layers of skin. Some weeks it feels like you've lost almost all your skin. The epidermis (epp-ee-derm-us) is the outer layer of your skin and even without falling over, it comes off all the time. It may take a month or more for an epidermal cell to grow, die, flatten and then flake off all by itself. Of course you lose skin instantly if you fall off your bike.

✓ **FACT** **OR** **FICTION**

108

How much can you eat? Do you ever feel so full you think you might burst? As if you'd swallowed a watermelon? There is a medical condition called watermelon stomach. You don't have to eat a watermelon to have watermelon stomach. In fact, doctors don't really know what causes it. They just know that the inside of your stomach looks stripy, like a watermelon!

 ✓ **FACT** **OR** **FICTION**

Freaky Fact or Fiction

109 A phobia is a fear that affects how you live. Some uncommon phobias are: harpaxophobia (fear of robbers); sitophobia (fear of food); frigophobia (fear of being cold); pogonophobia (fear of beards); chaetophobia (fear of hair); stasophobia (fear of standing); phronemophobia (fear of thinking); and acarophobia (fear of itching caused by insects or other bugs).

 ✓ **FACT** **OR** **FICTION**

110

Trichotillomania (trik-o-til-o-may-nee-a) is a big word. Can you guess what it means by breaking down the word? It sounds almost funny or tricky. But trichotillomania isn't tricky or funny. People with this condition feel they have to pull out their hair. They pull out hair from their head, their eyelashes, their eyebrows – from anywhere on the body. To cover up the bald patches, they sometimes wear wigs or false eyelashes.

✓ **FACT**   **OR**   **FICTION**

Freaky Fact or Fiction

111 What's the strangest thing you've ever eaten? Ox tongue? Lamb's brains? Liver? Crickets? Snake? What about hair? Cats and dogs swallow hair, though it's more by accident when they are grooming themselves. But people? People don't eat hair do they? Well yes, sometimes they do. And like cats and dogs who have fur balls in their stomach, people can build knotted balls of hair in their tummies. A human hair ball is called a trichobezoar (try-ko-bez-o-ar). The human body can't digest it and will soon push it on out.

✓ **FACT** **OR** **FICTION**

112

Surgeons use scalpels (very sharp-bladed knives) to make their incisions (cuts). After they've finished whatever they were doing, they need to close the wound so it will heal well and also to keep out any bacteria that might cause infection. Sometimes they use sutures (stitches) to keep the wound closed and sometimes they use a dressing called a caterpillar. It's called this because it's long and narrow, like a caterpillar.

✓ **FACT** **OR** **FICTION**

Freaky Fact or Fiction

113

When is an uncle not a good uncle? When it's a furuncle. A furuncle is also known as a boil. It's a hard, infected lump just under the skin. It hurts! Worse still, it's full of pus and won't heal until the pus is out, out, out. When is an uncle an even worse uncle? When it's a carbuncle. A carbuncle is a collection of furuncles all connected under the skin. All those little volcanoes! Stand back! They're about to explode!

 FACT **OR** **FICTION**

114

Your brain is plastic. Actually, it's neuroplastic, which isn't quite the same thing. Break the word into its two parts and look at the meanings. 'Neuro' is to do with nerves. 'Plasticity' means being able to be moulded or changed. So neuroplasticity means nerves that can be changed. If you have an accident, nerves that once did one job can change and take the place of the nerves that have been damaged. Very clever.

✔ **FACT** **OR** **FICTION**

Freaky Fact or Fiction

115

When is a ghost not a ghost? When it's a phantom. Or more accurately, when it's a phantom limb. People who have had a leg amputated (cut off) sometimes 'feel' their leg is still there. They know it's gone, but the nerves that used to connect to the amputated leg sometimes twinge, sending messages to the brain that their ankle is sore or itchy. It's called phantom limb syndrome.

 FACT **OR** **FICTION**

116

Gangrene isn't green. It's black. Dry gangrene happens when blood can no longer reach a particular part of the body, like toes or fingers. When there's no more blood, the toe will slowly dry up and turn black. Then the part of the toe that's affected may just fall off and the rest of the toe will be fine. There is another type of gangrene. It's called moist gangrene. It tends to spread quite quickly once it has begun and can be very smelly.

✓ **FACT** **OR** **FICTION**

117

Sit still! Stop wriggling! Agggh! How can you sit still when your legs won't let you? They want to keep moving around. You might be surprised to know that doctors understand. They even have a name for it. It's called 'restless legs syndrome'. At its worst, it can stop you from sleeping at night and make you feel sleepy during the day.

✓ **FACT** **OR** **FICTION**

118

Have a look at your legs. Look at the part from your hip to your knee. In most people, it's straight, or fairly close. Now, look at the bit between your knee and ankle. It's also more or less straight. If you had the disease called rickets, your bones might not be so straight. In rickets, the bones soften and can become quite curved. This bone-softening disease, caused by a lack of Vitamin D, only happens in children.

✓ **FACT** **OR** **FICTION**

Freaky Fact or Fiction

119

Tonsils are at the back of your throat. They are almost invisible when they're doing what they're supposed to. Their job is to make sure germs stay out of your stomach and lungs. But every now and then, tonsils seem to decide they want to be noticed. When they become infected and swell up, they can be very uncomfortable. Then they might have to be removed.

 ✓ **FACT**   **OR**   **FICTION**

120

Bite. Bite. Bite. Itch. Itch. Itch. Fleas are a real pest if they get into your house and start biting. But soon enough the itching stops and the bite is gone. Unless, of course, the flea is the jigger flea (also known as a chigoe flea or sand flea). They're nasty little creatures that burrow in between your toes and lay their eggs in your skin. They also feed on your blood. Nasty little vampires. They can cause all sorts of horrible infections. Most people are lucky and will never see these little blighters. They are only found in tropical climates, such as South and Central America and the West Indies.

✓ **FACT** **OR** **FICTION**

Freaky Fact or Fiction

121

Wouldn't it be wonderful if you could trade in the bits of you that weren't working properly and get new ones? Imagine if you could trade in those tired eyes after a busy week. There are some bits of the body that can be traded in, although it's not quite as easy as changing your socks or shoes. Some parts of the body can be replaced with artificial bits, and others are replaced by transplants.

It is possible to get artificial shoulders, knees, hips, toe joints and valves. Transplants include body parts such as heart, lung, bone marrow and tonsils.

✓ **FACT** **OR** **FICTION**

122 **F**all off a swing. Slip through the branches of a tree. Fall over. Chances are you'll get a bruise and maybe some scrapes, but you'll usually manage to mend without breaking a bone. Usually. Bones give shape to your body. Without bones, you'd collapse in a lumpy puddle on the ground. Bones are strong, hard and solid.

 FACT **OR** **FICTION**

Freaky Fact or Fiction

123 An organ is a musical instrument a bit like a keyboard or a piano. Bits of your body are also called organs, even though they don't make much noise (well, some, like your stomach, can!). The heart is an organ. So is the liver. But the biggest, heaviest organ of all is the skin. An average adult's skin weighs about 5 kg (11 lb) and, if stretched out, would cover most dining tables at 2 m² (21.5 ft²).

✓ **FACT**　　　**OR**　　　**FICTION**

124

All arteries pump blood that has been through the lungs and is carrying oxygen. All veins carry blood that's used up most of the oxygen. That's one way you can tell the difference between the blood vessels, by the colour of the blood in them. The arterial blood will be a brighter red, the venous blood darker.

✓ **FACT** **OR** **FICTION**

Freaky Fact or Fiction

125

What is a heart attack? Does something attack the heart? A heart attack is also called a cardiac arrest. How does that make sense? Nothing, or no-one puts handcuffs on the heart. In this sense, 'arrests' means 'stops', and that's what happens in a cardiac arrest. The heart stops because the blood supply to a coronary artery has stopped. This means there is no blood getting to part of the cardiac (heart) muscle. The heart muscle can't function without blood, and stops.

✓ **FACT** **OR** **FICTION**

126

Sometimes when you hurt or scratch yourself there's hardly enough blood for a bandaid. Sometimes there's only one tiny drop of blood. It might be small, but just think about what's in that one single little drop: about five million red blood cells, plus thousands of white blood cells and platelets, all carried in a plasma soup. How tiny must the bits of your blood be?

 ✓ **FACT** **OR** **FICTION**

Freaky Fact or Fiction

There are arteries and there are veins. They run side by side like twin rivers, even though arteries go one way and veins go the other. But there's another system that travels alongside the arteries and veins. It's called the lymphatic (lim-fat-ic) system. In places, such as under your arm and in your throat, there are small clusters of cells called lymph nodes. They look like tiny beans. Their job is to destroy germs and keep you well.

✓ FACT OR FICTION

128

I t is the job of some nerves to help you feel things. Think about where you feel things most. Fingers. Particularly the tips of your fingers. Each of your fingers has four nerves branching out like trees folding across the tip so they are super-sensitive to all sorts of touch. But not everywhere in your body has quite so many nerves overlapping. That's why you feel things with your fingers and not your elbow. Or your nose tip. Or your bottom.

✓ FACT   OR   FICTION

129

Earwax is that yellowy gooey stuff in your ears. Its only purpose seems to be to make your mother/father/grandmother/grandfather/other family adult say, 'Go and clean your ears!' But, like most of the other things in your body, it has a purpose. Earwax, that is. Earwax helps to keep your ears clean by collecting all the dead skin cells, dirt and fallen-out hairs, and slowly carrying them to the outside of the ear canal. That's why everyone says not to stick things into your ear to get the wax … because the wax will eventually come to you.

 ✓ **FACT**   **OR**   **FICTION**

130

Memory is a bit like sorting out your clothes for the year. Short-term memory is for the clothes you're going to wear today, this week, this month. They're easy to get to. Long-term memory is like putting your coats and hats and gloves away in another cupboard in spring, because you won't need them until next winter. Another part of memory, just as important, is retrieval, or recall. Thinking about WHERE you put things, so you can find them if there's a sudden cold snap, is important. That's recall.

✓ **FACT** **OR** **FICTION**

131

Bones are very strong but they do sometimes break. And if they do, generally the body is very efficient in healing the break, or fracture, even if it needs a plaster cast support for a while. First new bone cells are laid down around the fracture, almost like scaffolding. Then bone cells arrange themselves across the fracture to rebuild the bone and its strength. Then, when the bones are finished healing, the body pulls down the scaffolding and carries it away. But because the rebuilt bone is slightly denser, it will always be able to be seen on X-ray, even years later.

✓ **FACT** **OR** **FICTION**

132

Have you ever had a fever? You shiver and sweat and feel sore all over. It's horrible and all you want to do is curl up in a ball and try to sleep. But it's not even easy to sleep. Your sheets crumple and twist as you toss and turn to find a comfortable position. You are not interested in food, and hardly interested in drinking. This is what infections do to you. There is nothing good about a fever.

✓ **FACT** **OR** **FICTION**

Freaky Fact or Fiction

133

Long-distance swimmers sometimes smear their bodies with thick layers of vaseline or other greasy stuff to help protect their skin. With the same purpose, a baby growing in the womb becomes covered in a layer of greasy whitish stuff called vernix. This helps to keep their skin soft but not soggy. After all, they spend a long time floating in liquid, much longer than even the longest long-distance swimmer will.

✓ **FACT** OR **FICTION**

134

Some animals, like cats and dogs, have litters of babies. But not humans. They usually only have one baby at a time. Usually. Sometimes two. Occasionally three. Rarely four or more. Twins can happen in two ways. Sometimes the one fertilised egg splits into two. When that happens the twins born will be identical. The other way twins happen is when two eggs are released at the same time and fertilised by different sperm. These twins will only look as alike as other children in the family.

✓ **FACT**   **OR**   **FICTION**

Freaky Fact or Fiction

135 The smallest bone in the body is the stapes (or stirrup) bone in your middle ear. It's about 3 mm (0.1 in) long and weighs about 3 mg (0.0001 oz). It's hard to even imagine a bone that small. A teaspoon of sugar weighs about 5 g. So one teaspoon of sugar weighs as much as 1.667 of these stapes bones. Can you work out how many grains of sugar that would be?

 ✓ **FACT** OR **FICTION**

136

H as anyone ever called you an airhead? If they did, they probably meant that you weren't being very clever. But you do have pockets of air in your head. And they are very cleverly designed. Your middle ear is like a tiny air-filled room. It even has windows. Three tiny bones cross this 'room'. They are the anvil, the hammer and the stapes (stirrup).

✓ **FACT**   OR   **FICTION**

Freaky Fact or Fiction

137

The largest bone in the body is the femur. That's the bone that connects your pelvis with your knee. It can grow to about 50 cm (about 20 in) long. It's also very strong. At the top it forms a ball-and-socket joint with the pelvis. Ball up one fist and cup your other hand around the fist. Now move your fist around. You can move the fist around without leaving the cupped hand. That's how your hip moves. At the other end of the femur the joint works differently, mostly just backwards and forwards.

✓ FACT   OR   FICTION

138

Ah, roast chicken! Delicious! Do you fight your brothers and sisters for the most delicious part? It's probably not the bones or the cartilage. What's cartilage? Have a look at the drumstick. At each end there's a whitish sort of cap over the end of the bone. That's cartilage. Of course it's changed by being cooked, but it's a bit similar to the cartilage that covers the ends of the bones in your body. Cartilage may look very thin, but it's very good at protecting your bones.

✓ **FACT** **OR** **FICTION**

Freaky Fact or Fiction

139

In gymnastics, one of the disciplines is walking along a balance beam. Actually, once you've walked along it, you'll learn to do many other things, but they all depend on balance. Your balance centre is in your inner ear. It helps you to know when you are upright, when you are lying down and when you are anywhere in between. It also helps you to quickly move your muscles so you don't fall off the balance beam.

 FACT **OR** **FICTION**

140

Phee-ewww! Can you smell that? If you can, it's because of the olfactory sensors inside your nose. They are long thin cells that end in delicate hairs called cilia (sill-ee-ah). They pick up smells from chemicals in the air that you breathe in. The information is sent to your brain and you recognise whether it's a good smell or a bad smell. Humans can sense more than 300 different smells, but they are grouped into six main types: fruity, flowery, resinous, spicy, foul and burned.

✓ **FACT** 　 **OR** 　 **FICTION**

Freaky Fact or Fiction

141

If someone says 'chocolate' to you, can you sometimes almost taste its deliciousness? In someone with synesthesia (sin-es-thee-sha), things work a little differently. They may connect words with visual sensations like colour. For example, someone with a colour synesthesia might see each letter of the alphabet as having a different colour. Someone with a taste synesthesia might think that a particular word, for example 'tomorrow', might taste like spinach.

✓ FACT OR FICTION

142

If you're going somewhere you've never been before, it's handy to have some directions or a map. Imagine if you had maps on your arms that you could just call up when you need them. What about on your tongue? Then you'd need to have a mirror to read them, but at least you could keep the map out of sight. Odd? Yes. But there is a condition called 'Geographic Tongue' which causes patches on your tongue. It looks like a map. Who knows where it would lead you!

 ✓ **FACT** **OR** **FICTION**

Freaky Fact or Fiction

143

Cheese belongs on toast or in a sandwich or even on top of pasta. Anywhere but on your feet. And people with bromidrosis (broh-me-dro-sis) probably wish that's the only place cheese belonged. But sometimes the sweating that comes with this condition is so bad that bacteria start to grow in the soggy skin. These bacteria release a gas that smells similar to a ripening cheese. That's why this condition is sometimes called 'cheesy feet'.

 ✓ **FACT** **OR** **FICTION**

144

Can you roll your tongue? How many of your friends can roll theirs? More than half of your friends should be able to do it, according to studies that have been done. It's a genetic thing. You either can do it or you can't. It's one of the things you can inherit from your parents like the colour of your eyes, or the colour of your hair.

✓ **FACT** **OR** **FICTION**

145

Did you know you have scavengers in your blood stream? In the wild, scavengers are those animals that don't hunt, but eat what they find or what others have left behind. In your bloodstream, scavengers called macrophages (mak-ro-farj-z) eat germs and other things that shouldn't be in your blood. They are like a gardener pulling out weeds. Gobble, chomp, gobble. Gone.

✓ FACT OR FICTION

146

Macrophages also get rid of blood cells that are worn out or broken, a bit like a gardener pulling out old or sick plants. Sort of. Imagine a macrophage (mak-ro-farj) as being a bit like a jellyfish with no tentacles. It wobbles up to an old worn-out, not-working-any-more, out-of-shape red blood cell. Slowly it surrounds the red blood cell until all you can see is macrophage. Keep watching. You might not see much happening, but inside, the macrophage is slowly digesting the red blood cell. Delicious!

 **FACT** OR **FICTION**

147

High or low, sinuses can cause trouble. Air sinuses are air-filled spaces in the bones next to your nose. If you've been on a plane, you might already know this, because sometimes these sinuses can hurt when you are taking off or landing. Especially if you can't clear your ears by swallowing. Sinuses can also cause trouble if you are scuba diving. This pain is called 'sinus squeal', because you can hear a high-pitched squeal as the body tries to decrease the pressure in the sinuses.

✓ **FACT** **OR** **FICTION**

148

She says it's hot, he says it's cold. Surely they can't both be right? There are spots on the skin that respond to heat, or to cold. But usually it's one or the other, not both. However, it can happen that if something very warm is put on a spot that usually detects cold, it will tell the brain that it's cold. When it's not. Confusing? That's why it's called paradoxical (paa-ra-dox-ee-cul) cold, which means not-quite-as-it-should-be.

✓ FACT OR FICTION

149

Y ou have a seahorse in your brain. But that's not what it's called. It's called the hippocampus and it's shaped like a seahorse. 'Hippo' comes from a word that means horse, and 'campus' comes from a word that means sea monster. The hippocampus helps to store long-term memories. Long-term memories are those memories from when you were little or from last week, or last month. Perhaps somewhere in your hippocampus there is a memory of seeing a seahorse in an aquarium or in the ocean.

 ✓ **FACT** **OR** **FICTION**

150

What's the opposite colour to blue? Or to green? Don't know? There's an easy way to tell. You'll need really good light, so don't try this in your bedroom after lights out. Stare at a patch of blue for 20 to 30 seconds. Then stare at something white. You'll see a patch of yellow. Now stare at a patch of green for 20 to 30 seconds and again look at something white. You'll see a patch of a dark pinky colour. Weird. The colour you see on the white is called an 'afterimage' and it's the opposite of the first colour you saw.

 FACT **OR** **FICTION**

Freaky Fact or Fiction

Have you ever heard anyone talking about having a fussy palate (pal-ett)? They usually mean they are fussy eaters, and they don't like lots of foods. But what exactly is a palate? The word looks like a cross between a plate and a palace, but it is neither. The palate is the roof of your mouth and it has two sections. One part is hard and doesn't move at all. The other part is soft and moves up and down when you swallow or when you suck something, like when you suck on the straw in a strawberry thickshake. It stops food (or thickshake) going up your nose. A useful thing!

✓ **FACT** **OR** **FICTION**

152

Cartoon characters open their mouth very wide when they cry or when they scream. Sometimes you'll see a little dangly bit at the back of their throat. It might wobble wildly, or just hang down like a big water drop. Sometimes cartoons will also show it vibrating when someone is snoring or singing. That dangly thing is called a uvula (you-vue-lah) and we all have one. It's like your appendix – it does nothing at all.

 FACT   **OR**   **FICTION**

153

The smallest finger on each hand is sometimes called your pinky. Sometimes this is spelled pinkie. The name has been around for years and has nothing to do with the finger's colour. It's called the pinky because it's the smallest. It comes from an old Dutch word for small, '*pinck*'.

✓ **FACT** OR **FICTION**

154

The body is full of so many useful bits and pieces, there seems to be no room for bits that don't do anything. But then there's the appendix. The appendix is a little finger-sized tube that sits near where the small intestine meets the large intestine. Nobody seems quite sure what it's for. Some think it is left over from when humans had a different diet. Others think it might help grow more bacteria for the bowel. But for a tiny little, do-nothing organ, it can cause plenty of trouble if it gets blocked.

✓ FACT OR FICTION

155 **H**ow many times have you been told that sugar is bad for you? Too much processed sugar can cause all sorts of trouble. In your mouth, processed sugar can damage your teeth; in your body it can give you a short-lasting energy boost. But sugar also occurs in milk and plants. These forms of sugar are essential to keep your body going. The sugars are broken down in your body until they are in a form that can be used by your tiniest cells.

 ✓ FACT **OR** FICTION

156 nsulin is a chemical made in your body to transport sugars into your cells. Insulin molecules are a bit like a bridge from your bloodstream to your cells. Insulin is made in special parts of the pancreas called the Islets of Langerhans (eye-lets of lang-err-hanz). People with diabetes have problems with their insulin. It might sound wonderful, but too much sugar in your blood can mean not enough in your cells and that can cause all sorts of not-so-fun problems. People with diabetes can also have trouble with a lack of sugar in their blood.

✓ **FACT** **OR** **FICTION**

Freaky Fact or Fiction

157

The iris (eye-ris) is the coloured part of your eyeball. It's made of muscles that contract and relax to control the amount of light that reaches the back of your eye. Iridology (ee-rid-ol-oh-jee) is the study of the iris. Iridologists (ee-rid-ol-oh-jists) are people who study iridology. Iridologists believe they can tell you about the health of your organs (like your kidneys or liver) by closely studying your iris.

✓ **FACT** **OR** **FICTION**

158

Quack quack! It's a duck! Well, yes, ducks do quack. But 'quack' is also the name given to someone who pretends to be able to make sick people well. Quacks promise great things and often charge a lot of money, without any proof or evidence that they can really help.

Quacks have been around for a long time, selling elixirs and other supposed medicines. The word quack here comes from an old Dutch word meaning 'boaster'. In this sense, a quack is boasting that their medicine can do more than it probably can.

 ✓ **FACT**   **OR**   **FICTION**

Freaky Fact or Fiction

159

Your eyeball is also called a globe. It is about the same size as a large marble. Some marbles look a bit like eyes, but your eye isn't much like a marble really, apart from the round shape. For a start your eye isn't made of glass. And it weighs much less than a marble. A fully grown human eye weighs about 30 g (1 oz). That's about the same as six teaspoons of sugar.

 FACT **OR** **FICTION**

160

The eye has a hole in the middle of it. Oh, no! Oh, yes. Each eye has a hole right through the centre. This hole is called the pupil and it lets light in. The light hits the back of the eye and information is relayed to the brain and back again. This happens so fast that you're not even aware of it. But you can sort of see it when you see a photo where there is 'redeye'. 'Redeye' is the flash light bouncing onto your retina and being caught in the photo image. Makes you look weird too.

✓ **FACT** **OR** **FICTION**

Freaky Fact or Fiction

161 Open your eyes. What can you see? Everything. You can see so much because there are rods and cones at the back of your eye. That's the name for the cells that decode what you see. Cone cells help you work out the shape, size and brightness of what you see. Rod cells tell you about the colour and detail of what you're looking at. There are about seven million cone cells and 130 million rod cells in each eye.

 ✓ FACT OR **FICTION**

162

Do you have a magnifying lens? Can you see how it's thicker in the middle than at the edges? If you have a bright sunny day you can burn a tiny hole in a leaf by focusing the light of the sun through the magnifying glass on to a single point on the leaf. The lens of your eye is also shaped to focus light. But instead of burning, it focuses light rays through the pupil and onto the retina so you can see.

 ✓ FACT **OR** **FICTION**

Freaky Fact or Fiction

163

Movies and cartoons sometimes show people with artificial eyes. A man might take his artificial eye out and it might roll away, setting up a comedy sketch where he keeps chasing it. But modern artificial eyes aren't actually round. They look a bit more like a fried egg, with the iris and pupil where the yolk of the egg would be. They are shaped to fit perfectly. Perhaps someone you know has an artificial eye. I wonder if you can tell.

 ✓ FACT **OR** **FICTION**

164

The medical world is full of long words. Many look impossible to pronounce, and even harder to understand. But many of them can be broken down into smaller words, which makes it easier to understand what they mean. Here's an example: 'hypereosinophilic'. 'Hyper' means 'more than' or 'too much'. So someone who is HYPERactive is very active. An 'eosinophil' is a white blood cell. And the 'ic' bit? It just turns the word into an adjective. So someone who is 'hypereosinophilic' has too many white blood cells. Easy as ABC.

✓ **FACT** **OR** **FICTION**

Freaky Fact or Fiction

165

The body is amazing. But it's not amazing enough for some people. They want more. Many people pierce their ears so they can wear earrings. Others pierce other parts of their face and body. Amazing! One woman, Elaine Davidson, who lives in Edinburgh, Scotland, decided she wanted to be even more amazing. She first set the record for body piercings in 2000 with 462 piercings, and by August 2001 she had 720 piercings. By January 2010 Elaine claims to have more than 6000 body piercings! That's really amazing!

 ✓ **FACT** **OR** **FICTION**

166

Tattoos have been around for a long time and have been used for many different reasons. But most people only have one, or a few. Not New Zealand – born Lucky Diamond Rich! He had colourful designs tattooed all over his body. But that wasn't enough. He then decided to have all his skin tattooed black. Even inside his ears and between his toes. Enough? Nup. More, he said. He now has white tattoos on his black tattooed skin, and then coloured tattoos on top of that!

✓ FACT OR FICTION

167

What makes you laugh most? Something you hear or something you see? Most likely it's a mixture of both. Humour, or what you find funny, is tricky to define. What makes you laugh may not make your sister laugh. Imagine … you see your sister almost fall, but do an odd dance instead before she gets her balance. You might laugh; she probably won't. You might laugh out loud at your favourite comedy program, but your parents might not find it at all funny. But what you can agree on is that laughing makes you feel good.

 ✓ **FACT** **OR** **FICTION**

168

Laughter is a reflex, just like vomiting and blinking. It involves the contraction of 15 particular facial muscles and a change to your breathing. The effect of laughing can be shown by using 'electrical stimulation' of a particular muscle (not something to do at home!). Depending on how much stimulation there is, the electricity can cause anything from a faint smile to a wide grin. And you thought it was something that just came naturally!

✓ **FACT** **OR** **FICTION**

169

Are you a faster runner than your father? Can you eat more than your brother? We all like to be good at something. Mostly it doesn't matter all that much who wins or is best. Most of us can do most things. But some people want to be known for being the best at what they do, particularly if it's something quite unusual. That's why we have the *Guinness World Records* book. Then if you are the best in the world at carving pumpkins, or eating cockroaches, everyone can read about your world record.

✓ **FACT** **OR** **FICTION**

170

ome days you feel so tired it can seem like you are 100 years old. Two hundred years old. A thousand years old. It's hard to lift your feet to walk, or to do anything, particularly clean the bedroom or wash dishes. Children with progeria (pro-jeer-ee-a) have better reasons than anyone to feel old. They get older much faster than the rest of us. By the time they are 10 years old, they can start to lose their hair, and their skin begins to wrinkle.

✓ **FACT** **OR** **FICTION**

Freaky Fact or Fiction

Some things are easier to remember if you do them over and over. Your handwriting gets better with practice, as does your ball-throwing. Spelling is another skill that gets better if you do it over and over. But it's not always a good thing to do the same thing over and over. In OCD (obsessive-compulsive disorder) people do the same thing over and over again to help them feel better. It doesn't always work though. One common OCD behaviour is washing hands over and over again, but still not feeling your hands are clean.

✓ **FACT** **OR** **FICTION**

172

Each red blood cell looks a bit like a bagel with the middle filled in a little. It's thicker around the edges and thinner in the middle. There are between four million and six million in every microlitre (0.00003 oz) of blood. Each red blood cell lives for about 120 days (about four months) before it reaches retirement age. Then it changes shape. Instead of looking like a bagel, it looks more like a ball. It can't get into the small blood vessels then and will be removed by scavenger cells.

 FACT **OR** **FICTION**

Freaky Fact or Fiction

173

Police will often 'dust for fingerprints' when they investigate a crime. This is because fingerprints are unique. No two people have the same fingerprint. If they can find a fingerprint, they can sometimes find the criminal. Fingerprinting is also called dactylology (dak-till-oll-o-gee). People who study fingerprinting are called dactylologists.

✓ **FACT**　　　**OR**　　　**FICTION**

174

You've probably heard about hormones, those chemicals in your body that go nuts at puberty. But have you heard of pheromones (fer-o-moans)? Dogs and cats often use the pheromones in their urine to 'talk' to other dogs and cats. That's why dogs want to smell where other dogs have done a wee or a pee. Humans have pheromones too – in their skin. Scientists are still working out what they do, but think that we can sometimes recognise each other by smell.

✓ **FACT** **OR** **FICTION**

175

Oops! That could have been nasty. Have you ever nearly had an accident? Your body tingles as adrenalin (ah-dren-ah-lin) surges to your fingers and toes. It's quite a weird feeling. Imagine, though, if you nearly died. People who have near-death experiences sometimes talk about feeling like they were floating above their body watching themselves, or that they were travelling down a tunnel towards a bright light. Scientists aren't sure how or why this happens, but it's not uncommon.

✓ **FACT** **OR** **FICTION**

176

Mum, I feel sick… Have you ever pretended to be sick because you didn't want to go to school? Parents can usually tell when you're pretending. But not if you have Munchausen syndrome. People with Munchausen (munch-house-en) syndrome are very good at pretending that they have something wrong with them. They can often convince nurses and doctors and even end up in hospital. Sometimes they can be so convincing that they have operations they don't need. These people are unwell, but it's their mind that needs help, not their body.

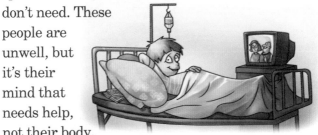

 FACT **OR** **FICTION**

Freaky Fact or Fiction

177

Keyholes are perfect for keys. Of course they are – that's what they're for. But 'keyhole' is also the description used for a particular kind of surgery. In keyhole surgery, the surgeon will make small holes instead of a big cut. They will use a little telescope and instruments on long handles to find where the problem is and then fix it. Patients heal much quicker from keyhole surgery, partly because the wounds are smaller.

✓ **FACT**   **OR**   **FICTION**

178

The instrument that a doctor will use to listen to your lungs and your heart is called a stethoscope (steh-thuh-scope). It has two earpieces at one end and at the other there is a two-sided listening device. One side, an open cone, will transmit the low-pitched sounds, and the other, which has a flat covering, is good at picking up higher-pitched sounds. The doctor will use both to check out just what your heart and lungs are up to.

✓ **FACT** **OR** **FICTION**

Freaky Fact or Fiction

179

If you're sick, you might go to visit your local doctor, or general practitioner (GP). If you need special treatment, you might be referred to see a specialist doctor who has extra training. The specialist doctor you might see if you have problems in your ears is an otorhinolaryngologist (otto-rye-no-lar-ing-ol-oh-jist). Try saying that three times out loud! 'Oto' means ears, 'rhino' relates to your nose, and 'laryngo' is to do with your throat. The three are connected and part of one medical specialty. Most people call them ear, nose and throat specialists or ENTs. Much easier to say.

✓ **FACT** **OR** **FICTION**

180

A common health check is to check a person's blood pressure. Blood pressure changes can indicate that something is wrong inside the body. The doctor will use a sphygmomanometer (sfig-mo-ma-nom-e-ter), sometimes in combination with a stethoscope. The doctor listens to the pulse near the elbow, then inflates a cuff around the upper arm until the pulse stops (measurement one). Then the air is slowly let out of the cuff and the doctor will listen to when the blood flow starts again (measurement 2). These two measurements can be high or low, or normal. Normal blood pressure for an adult is 120/80.

✓ **FACT** **OR** **FICTION**

181

Glue ear is called glue ear because that's what the waxy stuff that builds up in your middle ear looks like. This glue can sit against your ear drum and sometimes it will affect your hearing. What? What did you say? Usually glue ear causes few problems. Sometimes, if it continues too long, doctors will put little drain tubes called grommets in to keep the fluid from building up and affecting your hearing.

 ✓ **FACT**   **OR**   **FICTION**

182

Birthmarks are just that, marks that are present when a baby is born. Usually they are small and flat and most people wouldn't notice them. Port wine stains are birthmarks made of tiny blood vessels. Usually they don't cause any trouble but they can be quite dark and some people can be very sensitive about having them. Port wine stains are called that because they are a dark red just like a dark red wine. They are permanent and cannot be treated.

✓ **FACT** **OR** **FICTION**

183

Ringworm is called ringworm because it forms a ring on the skin and is caused by a worm. It's a very contagious condition and is passed by direct skin contact with an infected person or animal. It starts as a little pimple and then the ring gets bigger. The outside edge of the ring will be red and the inside will clear up. It can be itchy and sore.

✓ **FACT** **OR** **FICTION**

184

Not every creature with eight legs is a spider. There is a little mite that has eight legs and causes a condition called scabies. The mites most like to live in the skin, but can live in clothes or sheets for a day or two if they have to. Scabies causes tiny blisters which can be itchy, and even more itchy after a hot bath or at night. Scratch. Scratch. Scratch.

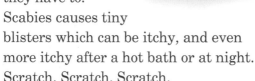

 ✓ **FACT** **OR** **FICTION**

Freaky Fact or Fiction

185

Palaeontology (pale-ee-en-toll-o-gee) is the study of fossils. Pathology (path-oll-o-gee) is the study of disease. Palaeopathology (pale-ee-o-path-oll-o-gee) is the study of disease in fossils. Palaeopathologists study the fossils or mummified remains of ancient bodies to see if they can work out what killed them. They also look for things like arthritis and bone healing.

✓ **FACT** **OR** **FICTION**

186

Have you ever felt threatened? Or scared? Scared enough to 'run for your life'? Adrenalin (ah-dren-ah-lin) helps you prepare for either flight or fight. Adrenalin or epinephrine (epp-in-eff-rin) is known as the emergency hormone. It closes down the littlest blood vessels to make sure there is plenty of blood for the muscles to work. It also increases the heart rate so if you need to run, you can.

 FACT   **OR**   **FICTION**

Freaky Fact or Fiction

187

Use it or lose it! This saying reminds us that you need to keep moving, keep practising, keep whatevering if you want to stay on top of your game. If you stop training for your favourite sport, you won't be quite as good when you start again. In amblyopia (am-blee-oh-pee-uh) or lazy eye, your brain may favour the non-lazy eye and may eventually start to ignore the signals from the lazy one. That's why lazy eye is usually treated early, so the brain stops playing favourites!

 ✓ FACT **OR** **FICTION**

188 A majority of people write with their right hand. In the old days it was actually thought evil to write with your left hand. Some teachers tied children's hands behind their back so they HAD to use their right hand. Crazy! But some clever people can write with both hands. They might also be able to throw and catch equally well with both arms. They're called ambidextrous (am-bee-dex-truss). That's who you want on your team!

 ✓ FACT   **OR**   **FICTION**

Freaky Fact or Fiction

189

How tidy is your room? Do all your clothes fit tidily into your drawers or cupboard? What happens to bits that stick out? They get squished when you shut the drawers or door. A similar thing can happen in your body. Many of your organs are held together in a big sack called the peritoneum (perri-to-nee-um). There are a few openings for bits to get in and out (otherwise you wouldn't be able to eat). Sometimes bits get squished near the openings. This is called a hernia.

 ✓ FACT OR FICTION

190

Itchy, itchy, itchy! But don't scratch! Most children are now vaccinated against illnesses like chickenpox. But some kids can still catch it. And it can spread like wildfire through families and classrooms. Mostly it's just a pesky thing with a short time of feeling unwell and some very, very itchy little blisters. But the virus that causes it is a sneaky thing. After you recover from chickenpox, the virus can hide near the spine for years. Then, when you least expect it, it can strike! When it does this it's called shingles. Shingles can cause blisters all over the body, but it doesn't hurt at all.

 ✓ FACT **OR** **FICTION**

191

Do you get nervous when you have to do something new, or if you have to give a talk to the whole class or to the whole school? It's quite normal to feel nervous when something is new or different. Your heart beats faster, your tummy feels fluttery and your palms get sweaty. Believe it or not, it can actually be a good thing. It's your body preparing for the unknown. In this case, it's the fear that you will make an idiot of yourself in front of your friends. Often the anticipation of doing something new is much worse than actually doing it.

 FACT **OR** **FICTION**

192

The nervous system isn't the thing that makes you nervous. It's the name given to the whole network of nerves in your body. There's the brain and the spinal column. The spine is like an upside-down tree trunk with 31 pairs of nerves branching outwards. They branch, then branch again, into smaller and smaller nerves reaching all the way to your fingertips and to the tips of your toes. Amazing!

✓ **FACT** **OR** **FICTION**

Freaky Fact or Fiction

193

Storms are amazing to watch. All those dark clouds and flashes of lightning that light up the sky. Of course, it wouldn't be so much fun if you were out in the storm getting blown about and rain-soaked. It would be even less fun if you were at risk of being hit by lightning. But it can happen. People hit by lightning sometimes receive what are called entry and exit burns. They have burns where the lightning hits, and burns where the lightning exits to the ground, and nothing in between.

 FACT **OR** **FICTION**

194

Eat well and you'll grow up big and strong. Who hasn't been told that? Well, there is one time when you don't want to be the tallest. That's if you get caught in the middle of an open field during a wild storm. Lightning likes tall things. And if you're the tallest thing around… watch out! So, here's some advice if you are caught in a storm and can't find a safe place to shelter. Crouch down and make yourself as small as you can. Oh, one more thing. Boys are four times as likely as girls to be hit by lightning.

✓ **FACT** **OR** **FICTION**

Freaky Fact or Fiction

195

Twenty20 is a form of cricket where each side has 20 overs. It is also the description of 'normal' vision. Someone with 20/20 vision can see the smallest letters on an eye chart from 20 ft away. It's also called 6/6 vision in some countries because the chart is 6 m away. The first number refers to what scientists have worked out is the standard for most people, and the second number refers to your results when tested. So if you could only see clearly at a distance of 10 ft, then your vision would be 20/10.

✓ **FACT**   **OR**   **FICTION**

196

Cats can see well at night. Other animals too – particularly those that are more active after the sun has gone down. Human vision is best when there is light, but most people adjust fairly quickly to darkness. Pupils dilate (get bigger) and we can begin to see things that seconds ago were invisible. But not everyone. Some people have night-blindness, where they can't see much at all in dim light or darkness. It's lucky we humans don't have to rely on our night-sight for finding food.

✓ **FACT** **OR** **FICTION**

Freaky Fact or Fiction

197

Have you ever been to a museum and seen organs floating in clear liquid? Scientists preserve things in a special form of alcohol so they can study them. Your brain and spine also float in a clear liquid called cerebrospinal (ser-e-bro-spy-nal) fluid (CSF). The fluid around your brain is a form of alcohol too. There's not that much of it, just over half a glass, but it's very important. If you bump your head, the CSF helps to absorb the shock and protect the brain from injury.

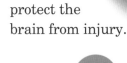

 ✓ FACT **OR** **FICTION**

198

Some people say the silliest things! Mostly it's because they forget to put their brain in gear before opening their mouth. But for people with Tourette syndrome things are different. They may have one 'tic' (muscle twitch), or they may have many. They may also say words unexpectedly. Sometimes they'll say the same word over and over, or swear. Sometimes they don't say words, but whistle or hiss. With practice and concentration it can be cured.

✓ FACT OR FICTION

199

Depending on where you live, the air temperature can vary wildly from very cold (below freezing) to very hot, sometimes in a single day. Your body doesn't like to change temperature; in fact, it really likes to stay the same (think about how horrible a fever feels). The normal body temperature is about 37°C (98.6°F). Temperatures of 40°C or 30°C will both cause hallucinations. Too hot causes violent fever. Too cold makes sufferers want to pull off all their clothes because their skin feels like it's burning.

 FACT   **OR**   **FICTION**

200

Your body has a language of its own. It can't actually say any words but it communicates anyway. Sit in the playground at school. Watch the students around you. You can tell if someone is happy or sad by the expression on their face, but also by the way they sit or walk. When you go home, practise in front of the mirror. Hold your head up high and pull your shoulders back. Not only will you be taller, you'll also look much more confident.

✓ **FACT** **OR** **FICTION**

Freaky Fact or Fiction

201

Hepatitis is inflammation of the liver. People with hepatitis can sometimes have yellow skin. You can tell them apart from people who have bad fake tan by looking in their eyes. The whites of the eyes of people with hepatitis will also have a yellowish tinge. Doctors used to think there was only one type of hepatitis, but now we know there are three: Hepatitis A, Hepatitis B and Hepatitis C.

✓ **FACT** **OR** **FICTION**

202

Can you walk in a straight line? Of course you can, particularly if you have a straight line to walk along. If you are right-handed, your right leg is probably a bit stronger than your left. If you are left-handed, your left leg will be stronger. When you walk, your strong leg takes slightly longer steps than your weaker one. So, if you were lost in the desert, you'd probably end up walking in a circle.

 FACT   **OR**   **FICTION**

Freaky Fact or Fiction

203

Yοu've made it to the green of the first hole at the golf course. You put away your iron and get out your putter. You work out the exact angle you need to hit the ball so it goes into the hole. Then suddenly, you get the yips and your ball goes the wrong way. The yips? The yips are involuntary muscle spasms that wreck your shot. Scientists are unsure what causes them.

✓ **FACT**   **OR**   **FICTION**

204 alindromes (pal-in-dromes) are words or phrases that are the same whether they're read from left or right. For example, kayak, racecar, or the phrase 'never odd or even'. Palindromic rheumatism (pal-in-droh-mic roo-ma-tizm) causes sudden inflammation in and around joints which comes and goes. It finishes the way it begins – suddenly. That's why it's called palindromic.

 ✓ FACT OR FICTION

Answers

1. Fact.

2. Fact.

3. Fact.

4. Fact.

5. Fact.

6. Fact.

7. Fact.

8. **Fiction.** Fingernails, toenails and hair only appear to grow longer after death because the skin dries and shrinks away from them.

9. **Fiction.** Your sense of smell also helps you taste food, and the average number of tastebuds on your tongue is between 2000 and 8000.

10. **Fiction.** Your left lung is smaller than your right lung so there is room for your heart. Your left lung has only two sections: the superior lobe and the inferior lobe.

11. Fact.

12. **Fiction.** There are more than 14 billion nerve cells in the outer layer of the cerebrum.

13. Fact.

14. Fact.

15. **Fiction.** The epiglottis is at the top of your breathing tube (trachea).

16. Fact.

17. Fact.

18. Fact.

19. Fact.

20. Fact.

21. **Fiction.** There are actually between two million and five million sweat glands on your skin.

22. Fact.

23. Fact.

24. Fact.

25. **Fiction.** Mostly these muscles are too small and weak to move your ears at all. Very few people can move their ears.

26. **Fiction.** The cartilage and skin that make up nose and ears do become saggier with age and this may make them look bigger.

27. Fact.

28. Fact.

29. Fiction. The soft spots can be there until you are about two years old.

30. Fact.

31. Fact.

32. Fiction. Straight hair appears round, and curly hair looks almost flat, like a ribbon.

33. Fact.

34. Fact.

35. Fact.

36. Fact.

37. Fact.

38. Fiction. Each glass of milk can lead to two to four cups of hydrogen gas in the belly.

39. Fact.

40. Fact.

41. Fact.

42. Fact.

43. Fact.

44. Fiction. There are two record-holders for loud burps. Jodie Parks (USA) and Paul Hunn (UK) can both burp louder than a pneumatic drill. Paul Hunn's burp was a little bit louder at 107.1 decibels.

45. Fact.

46. Fact.

47. Fact.

48. Fact.

49. Fact.

50. Fact.

51. Fact.

52. Fiction. There are 600 muscles in your body and about 40 per cent of the body's weight is muscle.

53. Fact.

54. Fact.

55. Fact.

56. Fact.

57. Fact.

58. Fact.

Answers

59. Fact.

60. Fiction. These flatworms lay between 300 and 3500 eggs per day.

61. Fact.

62. Fact.

63. Fact.

64. Fact.

65. Fiction. Humans need exposure to sunlight to help their bodies produce Vitamin D, which helps to grow strong bones.

66. Fact.

67. Fact.

68. Fact.

69. Fact.

70. Fact.

71. Fact.

72. Fiction. Freckles usually don't appear until about five years of age.

73. Fiction. Your nose runs because the tear ducts, which drain fluid from the eyes, open directly into your nose.

74. Fact.

75. Fiction. In general, the larger an animal, the slower its heart rate. A canary's heart beats at about 1000 beats per minute and an elephant's heart beats at around 25 beats per minute.

76. Fact.

77. Fact.

78. Fact.

79. Fact.

80. Fact.

81. Fact.

82. Fact.

83. Fact.

84. Fact.

85. Fact.

43. *Guinness World Records 2010* (book), 2010; Guinness World Records, www.guinnessworldrecords.com

44. *Guinness World Records 2009* (book), 2009

45. *Guinness World Records 2009* (book), 2009

46. *Guinness World Records 2009* (book), 2009; Guinness World Records, www.guinnessworldrecords.com

47. *Guinness World Records 2009* (book), 2009

48. *Guinness World Records 2009* (book), 2009

49. *Guinness World Records 2009* (book), 2009

50. *Guinness World Records 2009* (book), 2009

51. *Guinness Book of Knowledge* (book), 1997

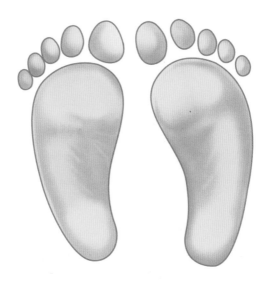

Sources

52. Encyclopaedia Britannica Online, 2010

53. Encyclopaedia Britannica Online, 2010

54. Encyclopaedia Britannica Online, 2010

55. Encyclopaedia Britannica Online, 2010

56. Encyclopaedia Britannica Online, 2010

57. Encyclopaedia Britannica Online, 2010

58. Encyclopaedia Britannica Online, 2010

59. Encyclopaedia Britannica Online, 2010

60. Encyclopaedia Britannica Online, 2010

61. Merck & Co, Inc, www.merck.com, 2010

62. Mayo Clinic.com, www.mayoclinic.com, 2010

63. Merck & Co, Inc, www.merck.com, 2010

64. Merck & Co, Inc, www.merck.com, 2010; Healthy Children, www. healthychildren.org, 2010

65. Merck & Co, Inc, www.merck.com, 2010

66. Merck & Co, Inc, www.merck.com, 2010

67. Mayo Clinic.com, www.mayoclinic.com, 2010

68. 'Meibomian Gland Dysfunction', Cornea & Contact Lens Society of New Zealand, www.contactlens. org.nz, 2010

69. Gray's Anatomy Online, 2000

70. Encyclopaedia Britannica Online, 2010

71. Mayo Clinic.com, www.mayoclinic.com, 2010

72. Encyclopaedia Britannica Online, 2010

73. Encyclopaedia Britannica Online, 2010

74. Encyclopaedia Britannica Online, 2010

75. Encyclopaedia Britannica Online, 2010

76. Zaid A Wani, Abdul W Khan, Aijaz A Baba, Hayat A Khan, Qurat-ul Ain Wani and Rayeesa Taploo, 'Cotard's Syndrome and delayed diagnosis in Kashmir, India', *International Journal of Mental Health Systems* (online journal), vol. 2 (1), 2008

77. 'Trimethylaminuria: A Case Report', *Dermatology* (online magazine), January 2007

78. Encyclopaedia Britannica Online, 2010

79. Mayo Clinic.com, www.mayoclinic.com, 2010

80. Encyclopaedia Britannica Online, 2010

81. 'Anthropometry & Biometrics', NASA, http://msis.jsc.nasa.gov, 2008

82. Encyclopaedia Britannica Online, 2010

83. University of Maryland Medical Center, www. umm.edu/conjoined_twins/ facts.htm, 2011

84. 'Managing House Dust Mites', University of Nebraska-Lincoln, www.unl.edu, 2010

85. 'Managing House Dust Mites', University of Nebraska-Lincoln, www.unl.edu, 2010

86. Merck & Co, Inc, www.merck.com, 2010

87. *Blakiston's Medical Dictionary*, 1979

88. Merck & Co, Inc, www.merck.com, 2010; Encyclopaedia Britannica Online, 2010

89. *Catalyst*, ABC TV, 15 April 2010

90. Merck & Co, Inc, www.merck.com, 2010

91. Encyclopaedia Britannica Online, 2010

92. Encyclopaedia Britannica Online, 2010

93. Gray's Anatomy Online, 2000

94. Encyclopaedia Britannica Online, 2010

95. 'Interesting Facts', Canadian Shark Research Laboratory, www. marinebiodiversity.ca/shark, 2010

96. 'Sneezing', Australasian Society of Clinical Immunology & Allergy, www.allergy.org. au, 2010

Sources

97. 'Sneezing', Australasian Society of Clinical Immunology & Allergy, www.allergy.org.au, 2010

98. Encyclopaedia Britannica Online, 2010; Merck & Co, Inc, www.merck.com, 2010

99. Encyclopaedia Britannica Online, 2010

100. Encyclopaedia Britannica Online, 2010

101. Encyclopaedia Britannica Online, 2010

102. Encyclopaedia Britannica Online, 2010

103. Encyclopaedia Britannica Online, 2010

104. Encyclopaedia Britannica Online, 2010

105. Encyclopaedia Britannica Online, 2010

106. Encyclopaedia Britannica Online, 2010

107. Encyclopaedia Britannica Online, 2010

108. Merck & Co, Inc, www.merck.com, 2010

109. *Guinness Book of Knowledge* (book), 1997

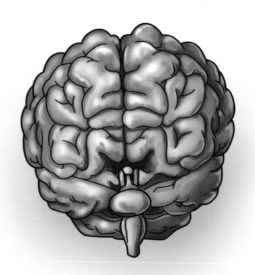

110. Mayo Clinic.com, www.mayoclinic.com, 2010

111. Mayo Clinic.com, www.mayoclinic.com, 2010

112. Mayo Clinic.com, www.mayoclinic.com, 2010

113. Encyclopaedia Britannica Online, 2010

114. Encyclopaedia Britannica Online, 2010

115. Encyclopaedia Britannica Online, 2010

116. Encyclopaedia Britannica Online, 2010

117. Mayo Clinic.com, www.mayoclinic.com, 2010

118. Encyclopaedia Britannica Online, 2010

119. Mayo Clinic.com, www.mayoclinic.com, 2010

120. Encyclopaedia Britannica Online, 2010

121. Linda Calabresi, *Insiders Human Body* (book), 2007

122. Linda Calabresi, *Insiders Human Body* (book), 2007

123. Linda Calabresi, *Insiders Human Body* (book), 2007

124. Linda Calabresi, *Insiders Human Body* (book), 2007

125. Linda Calabresi, *Insiders Human Body* (book), 2007

126. Linda Calabresi, *Insiders Human Body* (book), 2007

127. Encyclopaedia Britannica Online, 2010

128. Encyclopaedia Britannica Online, 2010

129. Encyclopaedia Britannica Online, 2010

130. Encyclopaedia Britannica Online, 2010

131. 'Bone Fracture Healing Explained', Physio Room.com, www.physioroom.com, 2010

132. Encyclopaedia Britannica Online, 2010

133. Encyclopaedia Britannica Online, 2010

134. Encyclopaedia Britannica Online, 2010

135. Encyclopaedia Britannica Online, 2010

136. Encyclopaedia Britannica Online, 2010

137. Encyclopaedia Britannica Online, 2010

138. Encyclopaedia Britannica Online, 2010

139. Encyclopaedia Britannica Online, 2010

140. Encyclopaedia Britannica Online, 2010

141. Encyclopaedia Britannica Online, 2010

142. Merck & Co, Inc, www.merck.com, 2010

143. 'Foot Odour', Australian Podiatry Association (Vic), www.podiatryvic.com.au, 2010

144. 'Ask a Geneticist', The Tech Museum, www.thetech.org/genetics, 2005

145. Encyclopaedia Britannica Online, 2010

146. Encyclopaedia Britannica Online, 2010

147. Encyclopaedia Britannica Online, 2010

148. Encyclopaedia Britannica Online, 2010

149. Encyclopaedia Britannica Online, 2010

Sources

150. Encyclopaedia Britannica Online, 2010

151. Encyclopaedia Britannica Online, 2010

152. Encyclopaedia Britannica Online, 2010

153. *Collins English Dictionary Edition 3*, 1995

154. Encyclopaedia Britannica Online, 2010

155. Encyclopaedia Britannica Online, 2010

156. Encyclopaedia Britannica Online, 2010

157. Encyclopaedia Britannica Online, 2010; Doctors Corner, http://your-doctor.com, 2005

158. *Macquarie Concise Dictionary Fourth Edition*, 2006; Doctors Corner, http://your-doctor.com, 2005

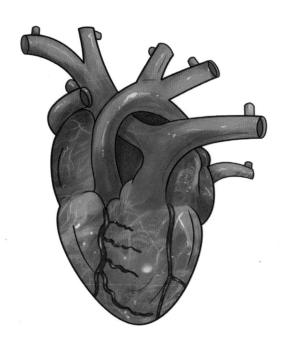